Loveland, Colorado

www.grouppublishing.com

The Gigantic Book of Games for Youth Ministry, Volume 2

Copyright © 1999 Group Publishing, Inc.

Visit our Web site: **www.grouppublishing.com**

Credits
Contributing Authors: Thomas J. Aron, Jay R. Ashcraft, Michael W. Capps, Karen Dockrey, Mike Gillespie, Monica K. Glenn, Debbie Gowensmith, Stacy Haverstock, Trudy J. Hewitt, Michele Howe, Mikal Keefer, Jan Kershner, Cortland Kirkeby, Trish Kline, Pamela Malloy, Kelly Martin, Ryan C. Nielsen, Lori Haynes Niles, Todd Outcalt, Siv M. Ricketts, Alison Simpson, Tim Simpson, and Dave Thornton
Book Acquisitions Editor: Amy Simpson
Editor: Debbie Gowensmith
Creative Development Editor: Dave Thornton
Chief Creative Officer: Joani Schultz
Copy Editor: Shirley Michaels
Art Director: Randy Kady
Cover Art Director: Jeff A. Storm
Cover Designer: Becky Hawley
Cover Photography: Corbis Images
Computer Graphic Artist: Nighthawk Design/Pamela K. Clifford
Illustrator: Matt Wood
Production Manager: Peggy Naylor

Library of Congress Cataloging-in-Publication Data
The gigantic book of games for youth ministry / [contributing authors, Thomas J. Aron...et al. ; editor, Debbie Gowensmith].
    p. cm.
   Includes indexes.
   1. Church group work with teenagers. 2. Games in Christian education. I. Aron, Thomas. II. Gowensmith, Debbie.
   BV4447.G54 1998
   259'.23—dc21

                                                    98-29467
                                                   CIP

ISBN 0-7644-2113-1 (v. 1)
ISBN 0-7644-2089-5 (v. 2)

10 9 8 7 6 5   08 07 06 05 04

Printed in the United States of America.

Contents

Contents

INTRODUCTION

"Game...Any form of play or way of playing; amusement, recreation; sport; frolic; play."

Play? Amusement? Frolic? Are these worthy pursuits for a Christian youth group? Though fun and games may seem frivolous, teenagers often reap hidden benefits from games. When your teenagers play games, they're not only taking a break from the stress in their lives, but they're also developing social skills. They're having fun with new people. They're learning about themselves.

Search Institute reports that in order to be socially competent, young people must understand how to work with others, hold their own against opponents, and anticipate what's coming (Dorothy L. Williams, "Essential for Survival on the Troubled Journey," Source newsletter, April 1991, from www.search-institute.org). While your regular program material may instruct kids on the fine art of social competence, games can help them develop that competence in a fun, informal environment.

That's why we've developed this second volume of *The Gigantic Book of Games for Youth Ministry*. This volume offers three categories of games to further strengthen your game repertoire: (1) Brain-Stretching, (2) Friend-Making, and (3) Holiday.

Brain-Stretching Games will challenge your youth in awareness, logic, reason, and creative problem solving. These games will encourage your kids to stretch and exercise their minds.

Friend-Making Games will allow your group members to get to know one another. Search Institute has found that "friend-making skill is one of the major essentials of life; without it, no matter how much else one knows, the journeyer finds more potholes and curves in the road than smooth, straight stretches" (Williams, "Essential for Survival on the Troubled Journey"). These games will break down barriers, provide opportunities for conversation, and allow teenagers to have fun together.

Holiday Games will give your group members reasons to celebrate—even for lesser-known holidays, such as Flag Day! These games will promote understanding about holidays and allow your kids to have a blast.

Use these games during meetings, retreats, outings, and travel. Use them to challenge your students mentally, to promote interaction, and to simply have fun. The three hundred games in this book provide a great variety of styles:

active, introspective, competitive, cooperative, team, individual, and so on. You'll find games to enhance almost any situation.

Just like the first volume, this book was created with you in mind. Each game includes several quick *at-a-glance* references: a game overview, a list of supplies, recommended group size, approximate playing time, and easy-to-understand directions. We've also included useful indexes of game types, group sizes, and times involved. If you need a game that requires no supplies and no preparation, check the game type index. If you'd like some game ideas for those long road trips, check the index for travel games. If you need a game for a large group of teenagers, check the group size index. If you have only five minutes to play a game, check the time index.

The Gigantic Book of Games for Youth Ministry, Volume 2 is a lot about playing, frolicking, and being amused. But right along with all that fun, your students will grow and learn. So let the games begin!

BRAIN-STRETCHING GAMES

Ad Campaign

Overview: Kids will create advertisements for new products.

Game Type: Funny, suitable for disabled

Group Size: 10 to 20

Time Involved: 10 to 20

Supplies: A watch

Preparation: None

Have kids get into groups of four, and tell them they're going to spend the next few minutes as the creative teams for an ad agency.

Say: **This ad agency is trying to sell a brand new product. Your job is to decide what the product is and to create an advertisement to introduce the product to the public. You'll have only six minutes to come up with the product and the ad. Also, the ad must be from thirty to forty-five seconds long, no shorter and no longer. Finally, you'll have to act out the ad for us, and everyone in your group has to somehow be a part of it.**

When everyone understands the rules, start timing the kids. After six minutes, have each group present its ad. As groups present, be sure to time them. After everyone has presented, have kids give themselves a hand. If you have time, have kids form new groups to play again.

Alphabet Game

Overview: Kids will hunt for objects that begin with every letter of the alphabet.

Game Type: Active

Group Size: Any

Time Involved: 10 to 20 minutes

Supplies: Large grocery sacks, pencils, paper, and a watch

Preparation: None

Have kids form teams of three or four. Give each team a large grocery sack.

Say: **Using the entire building, your team must find objects that start with every letter of the alphabet. You may have only one object per letter, and all the objects must fit inside your grocery sack. Also, you must remember or write down where you get each object so you can return it at the end of the game. You'll have exactly fifteen minutes to find all your objects and be back here. For every twenty seconds you're late, your team must forfeit one object.**

If you'd like kids to stay out of certain areas of the building, set them as out-of-bounds areas. Then start the game, and keep close track of time.

When all the teams have returned, go through the alphabet to see the ingenious objects they collected. Each object is worth one hundred points, so have teams keep track of their own points. After the game, make sure teams put back all the objects they collected.

ANCIENT NUMBERS

Overview: Kids will try to figure out the pattern to an "ancient numbering system."

Game Type: Quiet, suitable for disabled

Group Size: 2 to 10

Time Involved: 2 to 10 minutes

Supplies: Three short sticks

Preparation: None

Tell the kids that you've been studying an ancient style of numbering and that you'd like to see if they can figure out some of the numbers you've learned. Tell the kids that you're going to arrange three sticks in different patterns and that they have to figure out what the numbers are.

Squat down, and place the three sticks on the ground in a random fashion. Have kids gather around you, and ask them to really study the sticks and try to figure out what the number is.

The secret to this game is that as soon as you place the sticks on the ground, you should discreetly extend a certain number of fingers and keep them extended. For example, you might lean on your hands in such a way

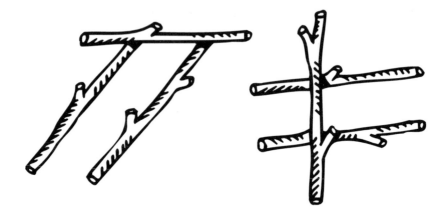

that you're actually extending two right fingers and three left fingers. After kids have studied the sticks for about ten seconds, tell them that "five" is the correct answer. Place the sticks in another random pattern, and discreetly extend two fingers. Again, ask kids if they know what number the sticks are forming. After a few seconds, tell them that the correct answer is "two."

Continue the process until the kids start to catch on. As some group members figure out the pattern, ask them to let the other kids figure it out for themselves. When all but about three people have figured out the pattern, allow a volunteer to explain the pattern to everyone.

ARE WE RELATED?

Overview: Kids will create lists of items so teams can figure out how the items are related.

Game Type: Knowledge-builder, quiet, suitable for disabled

Group Size: 10 to 20

Time Involved: 10 to 20 minutes

Supplies: Paper, pencils, and a watch

Preparation: None

Have kids form teams of five. Tell kids you're going to name a category and then each team is going to create a list of four things that are somehow related.

Say: **For example, if I name "geography" as a category, a team might list "oil wells, yellow roses, cowboy hats, and pickup trucks." Then the** other teams will have to figure out that the answer is "Texas" because you can find everything on the list in Texas.

Explain that the first team will say its list and the second team will have ten seconds to discuss the list and call out how the items are related. If the second team calls out the right answer, that team gets a point. If the team doesn't call out the right answer, the list goes to the third team (if there is a third team), and so on. If no one guesses the right answer, the first team gets a point. Then the second team gets to state its list for the third team (or the first team if there are only two teams), and so on. Caution kids that if a team lists really obscure, personal facts that no one could know, each of the other teams will get one point.

When everyone understands the rules, distribute paper and a pencil to each team. Then start the play by naming a category. Possible categories are geography, history, science, biology, music, fads, movies, and literature. Keep track of the points for each team, and play until every team has been able to state a list at least twice.

BABELING TOWER-BUILDERS

Overview: Kids will work together in teams to build towers while speaking only "baby talk."

Game Type: Funny, suitable for disabled, team-builder

Group Size: Any

Time Involved: 2 to 10 minutes

Supplies: Paper cups and index cards

Preparation: None

Have kids form teams of four, and give each team four paper cups and four index cards.

Say: **Using only these eight items, each team will attempt to build the tallest tower in five minutes. To add to the challenge, you may communicate with one another using only gestures and baby noises such as "goo-goo" and "gaa-gaa." Ready? Go!**

LEADER TIP

If you want to award a funny prize, bring four baby pacifiers for the winning team.

In five minutes, declare the team that built the tallest tower the winner.

BIBLE-PAIR CHARADES

Overview: Kids will act out famous Bible duos for the group to guess.

Game Type: Bible, knowledge-builder, suitable for disabled

Group Size: 10 to 20

Time Involved: 20 to 30 minutes

Supplies: Bibles, the "Biblical Duos" handout (p. 17), a watch, and scissors

Preparation: Make photocopies of the "Biblical Duos" handout (p. 17), and cut apart the duos.

Have kids form pairs, and give each pair a slip from the "Biblical Duos" handout (p. 17).

Say: **You have two minutes to read about your Bible characters and some of the activities in their lives. Then you'll pantomime it for the rest of the group to guess.**

Give kids a couple of minutes to prepare, and have Bibles available for kids to look up their characters. Then have each pair perform its pantomime while the rest of the group tries to guess who the pair is portraying.

Biblical Duos

Adam—Gardener, animal keeper

Eve—Snake talker, fruit eater

Cain—Farmer, jealous, murderer

Abel—Shepherd, murdered

Noah—Obedient, ark builder

Noah's Wife—Boat traveler

Abraham—Traveler, old father

Sarah—Doubter, aged mom

Moses—Leader, Red Sea parter

Aaron—Spokesman, brother

Samson—Strong man, fighter

Delilah—Temptress, hair cutter

David—Giant slayer, harp player, king

Bathsheba—Public bather

Peter—Fisherman, rock

Andrew—Fisherman, disciple

BIBLICAL TWENTY QUESTIONS

Overview: Kids will play Twenty Questions to try to figure out biblical events.

Game Type: Bible, knowledge-builder, no supplies and no preparation, quiet, suitable for disabled, travel

Group Size: Any

Time Involved: 20 to 30 minutes

Supplies: None

Preparation: None

LEADER TIP

You can use this game to review biblical events kids have studied. You can also use this game to introduce biblical events or characters to kids. To do so, you may want to let kids use Bibles during the game.

Explain to the kids that they're going to play Biblical Twenty Questions.

Say: **I'll think of a biblical event. Then each person will get a chance to ask a question that can be answered only with "yes" or "no." The group can ask only twenty questions. The object is to be the first person to figure out what the biblical event is. If you guess incorrectly, you can't guess again, but you can still ask questions.**

Begin the game and play several rounds.

BODY SPELLING

Overview: Kids will work together to use their bodies to spell words.

Game Type: Active, funny, outside, team-builder

Group Size: 50 to 75

Time Involved: 2 to 10 minutes

Supplies: A megaphone

Preparation: Select an area where the kids can be on a playing field and you can be above them—on a small hill or in bleachers above a football field, for example.

Have kids form teams of ten. Tell them you'll yell out a letter for teams to form on the field with their bodies—similar to a marching band—so you can see it from your vantage point.

When kids understand, have teams spread out on the field while you walk to higher ground. Then yell out a letter and have teams each form it. Then have some fun by beginning slowly, one letter at a time, then yelling letters more and more rapidly. When the group is ready, try words, assigning a different letter to each group. Use any word or phrase you wish; just keep the pace moving. A lot of mental and physical energy will be spent on this one!

CALL THE COLORS

Overview: Kids will be challenged to think quickly and clearly in order to recognize colors.

Game Type: Quiet, suitable for disabled

Group Size: 20 to 30

Time Involved: 10 to 20 minutes

Supplies: Three 18x24-inch sheets of poster board or cardboard, markers in eight basic colors, paper, a pencil, and a watch.

Preparation: This game requires up to forty-five minutes of preparation the first time, but you can use the supplies you make again and again.

In a line on a piece of poster board, print the *name* of each color, but use a marker in a color *different from* the color named. For example, you could use an orange marker to write the word "yellow," a green marker to write the word "red," a blue marker to write the word "brown," and so on. Print all eight words in this manner, and then repeat the words using different colors than you used before. For example, this time you could use a blue marker to write the word "yellow," an orange marker to write the word "red," and a red marker to write the word "brown." On each line, randomly select a color or two to name correctly. For example, you could use the color red to write the word "red." Continue until you've repeated the words three times, for a total of twenty-four words on one sheet of poster board. On the second and third sheets of poster board, repeat the process, but change the order of the words.

When you have finished this step, write a "key" in pencil on the back of each sheet of poster board to help you check the correct answers during the game. To do this, write the order in which the *colors*—not the words—appear, from left to right and line by line.

Have kids form teams of no more than five or six. Have each team line up in single file, facing you. Explain that you're going to hold up a sheet of poster board and allow the first person on the first team twenty seconds to name the order in which the colors appear—the colors, not the words.

Say: **For each correct color, the team will get one point. Then that person will move to the back of the team's line, and I'll move to the next team and repeat the process. We'll play until everyone has had an opportunity to read a sheet of poster board.**

LEADER TIP

With a large group, you might want to ask someone to monitor each person's time and record each person's score. Count the number of correct colors for each person, and call out the number before moving to the next team.

Start with the first person, and award one point for each correct color named. Go from team to team, and randomly change the sheets of poster board so no one memorizes the color patterns. Speed is essential to increase the fun and the challenge.

At the end of the game, if any teams have tied, continue the game for one more round. This time, have the kids name the colors backward.

CAN YOU BELIEVE THIS?

Overview: Kids will determine how to get two empty soda cans together without using their hands.

Game Type: Quiet, suitable for disabled

Group Size: 2 to 10

Time Involved: 2 to 10 minutes

Supplies: Two empty soda cans and fifteen straws

Preparation: None

Place the cans and straws on a table.

Say: **Your challenge is to set these empty soda cans three inches apart and get them to touch without falling over. You may use these straws but no other supplies. You may not move the cans with your hands or the straws after you've set up the cans.**

Let the kids talk about it and try different methods. Here's one solution: Line up the straws about one-half inch apart. Set the soda cans three inches apart on top of the straws. Blow between the cans until they touch. This works because the moving air between the cans exerts less pressure than the air on the sides of the cans.

VARIATION

For a different twist, begin the game with the cans together, and ask the kids to figure out how to get them to move apart.

Can't Buy a Vowel

Overview: Individually and as a team, kids will create as many words as possible.

Game Type: Quiet, suitable for disabled, travel

Group Size: Any

Time Involved: 2 to 10 minutes

Supplies: Slips of paper, sheets of paper, pens, and a watch

Preparation: None

Give each teenager a slip of paper and a pen. Without explaining the game's objective, have each person write down two different consonants and one vowel. Next have kids form teams of three, and give each team a sheet of paper. Have each team decide who will go first, second, and third.

Then say: **Those who are first have two minutes to write down as many words as you can from the three letters you selected. You may not repeat a letter in any word. For example, if you selected b, l, and e, you may not use the letter e twice to make the words "bee" and "lee." Ready? Go!**

After two minutes, ask the second team members to join the first; then they have two minutes to write down as many as words as they can create from their six letters. Again, they may not repeat a letter in a word unless both team members selected the same letter.

After two minutes, ask the third team members to join the first two and help create new words from the nine letters. After two minutes, call time. Have each team count the words they created.

Cereal Spelling Bee

Overview: Kids will see how many words they can spell with alphabet cereal.

Game Type: Food, suitable for disabled

Group Size: Any

Time Involved: 2 to 10 minutes

Supplies: Paper towels, a one-cup measuring cup, alphabet cereal, and a watch

Preparation: None

Hand each person a paper towel, and place one cup of alphabet cereal on each paper towel.

Say: **Using the cereal, spell as many words as you can in thirty seconds. You'll get two points for each word you spell, but only one point for a repeated word. For example, if you spell "ate," you'll get two points; if you spell "ate" again, you'll get only one point for the second "ate." You may use each piece of cereal only once, and the word "a" doesn't count. Ready? Go!**

After thirty seconds, call time. Have kids tally their points, and then play again. After the game, kids can munch on their cereal as a snack.

CHOCOLATE BARS FOR THE WORLD

Overview: Kids will divide a little bit of candy equally among the group members.

Game Type: Food, quiet, suitable for disabled

Group Size: 10 to 20

Time Involved: 2 to 10 minutes

Supplies: Chocolate bars, paper, and pencils

Preparation: Break the chocolate bars into pieces that look like the illustration below.

LEADER TIP
The chocolate bars will break and cut more easily if they're at room temperature. Cold chocolate bars are too brittle to break correctly.

Have kids form groups of four, and give each group one of the chocolate bar sections.

Say: **In your groups, figure out a way to divide your candy so that each person gets exactly the same amount. You might want to trace your candy onto a piece of paper and work the division out on paper before actually breaking the candy.**

Here's the answer:

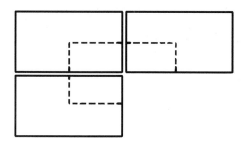

CLUCK, CLUCK, CHUCKLE, CHUCKLE

Overview: Kids will try to figure out who the "clown" is.

Game Type: Junior high, no supplies and no preparation, suitable for disabled, travel

Group Size: Any

Time Involved: 10 to 20 minutes

Supplies: None

Preparation: None

The object of this game is to figure out who the "clown" is. The secret to this game is that the clown is the first person to speak after you ask, "Who is the clown?"

Randomly point at teenagers while saying: **Cluck, cluck, chuckle, chuckle. Who is the clown?**

Ask kids to try to figure out who the clown is and why that person is the clown. When kids guess, tell them if they're correct. When kids guess correctly, ask them to whisper in your ear why that person was the clown. If they understand the game's secret, have them sit out and enjoy watching others try to figure out the game. If someone guesses incorrectly, tell the group who the real clown was and then continue the game.

Mix up the way you say, "Chuck, chuck, chuckle, chuckle" to throw the kids. If kids want a hint, tell them to listen carefully. Continue until everyone has figured out the secret or until they don't want to play anymore.

CONSTRUCTIVE RESPONSES AND POSITIVE SOLUTIONS

Overview: Kids will practice formulating positive solutions to problems.

Game Type: Discussion-starter, knowledge-builder, quiet, senior high, suitable for disabled

Group Size: 20 to 30

Time Involved: 30 to 45 minutes

Supplies: Newsmagazines and newspapers, scissors, paper, and pens

Preparation: None

Have kids form pairs; distribute magazines, newspapers, scissors, paper, and pens. Ask kids to look through the magazines and newspapers and each clip out an article about a tragic event or other bad news. Then have each pair analyze the article, asking who, what, when, where, and why about the story.

After a few minutes, challenge pairs to write down at least three positive solutions to the situation.

Say: **Your solutions may answer the questions "Where can the victims go from here?" or "What can other people do to help?" Just remember that we're not trying to place blame—we're trying to create solutions.**

After a few minutes, have kids pass the articles to you but hold onto their written responses. Choose a few articles to read aloud. After you read each article, ask the pair to read its solutions to the group. Then ask the group to add other solutions.

CRAZY CARDS

Overview: Kids will test their engineering skills as they battle the elements in this fast-paced (and sometimes frustrating!) house-of-cards relay.

Game Type: Outside, suitable for disabled

Group Size: 20 to 30

Time Involved: 2 to 10

Supplies: Small portable tables (card tables or plastic lawn tables work well), old playing cards (easily available at garage sales or thrift stores), glue or paper clips, and a watch

Preparation: Set up a table outside for each team. On each table, place glue or paper clips and a pack of old playing cards.

Have kids form two teams. If you have more than twenty kids, have them form three teams. Have each team line up in single file about six feet from its table. Explain that kids will take turns in relay fashion to see which team can build the tallest house of cards in five minutes.

Say: **Each player can add only two cards at a time. If the building falls down, the next player must begin again. Teammates may call out instructions and encouragement, but they may not help the player at the table in any other way.**

Because wind—even breezes—will be a factor, tell kids they can use the glue or paper clips to help stabilize their buildings. Then give teams a minute or two to develop an effective building strategy. They may decide to build a broad base to help stabilize the structure, or they may decide to go straight for height and hope for the best!

Start the relay. After five minutes, call time and see which team built the tallest card house.

EARTHQUAKE

Overview: Kids will work together to get everyone out of a room before it "collapses."

Game Type: Suitable for disabled, team-builder

Group Size: Any

Time Involved: 10 to 20 minutes

Supplies: A watch

Preparation: None

Have everyone lie down on the floor. Explain that an earthquake has just occurred and it knocked everyone to the floor. Tell kids that the earthquake's intensity caused part of the building to cave in, injuring every person in the room. Assign everyone an injury. For example, all boys with brown hair can't use their legs, all girls wearing jeans can't use their arms, and everyone with blonde hair can't see. Explain that the building is starting to collapse and everyone has to get out of the room within fifteen minutes.

Say: **You'll have to work together to get everyone out safely. If you use your strengths and coordinate your work, you'll accomplish your task.**

Start the game. After fifteen minutes, call time. Be sure to discuss with the kids what happened during the game.

ELECTRIC FENCE

Overview: Kids will try to get the entire group outside an "electric fence."

Game Type: Outside, team-builder

Group Size: 2 to 10

Time Involved: 20 to 30 minutes

Supplies: A yardstick, a rope, and four posts or tall chairs

Preparation: Measure a 15x15-foot area, and place the posts or
tall chairs in the corners. Then surround the area
with rope that's three to four feet off the ground.

Have kids get inside the roped-off area. Then tell them they have to figure
out how to get back outside the rope with some new rules. Explain that the
rope is a "fence" that emits an electric current from the rope to the ground,
so kids can't touch the rope or anything underneath it. Also, if anyone
touches the rope or anything beneath it, the whole group must start over.

Let the kids use their problem-solving skills to determine a way to get
everyone safely outside the fence. If they have trouble, suggest that they work
together to lift the bigger people out first and leave the smallest person to be
picked up last.

EVANGELISM HANDSHAKES

Overview: Kids will count handshakes to learn that evangelism
involves reaching out to others.

Game Type: Discussion-starter, mixer, suitable for disabled

Group Size: 30 to 50

Time Involved: 2 to 10 minutes

Supplies: None

Preparation: None

Have kids form teams of seven.

Say: **The object of this game is to shake hands with everyone on
your team. However, you may shake hands with each person only once.
After you've shaken hands with everyone, figure out how many handshakes actually occurred within your team. As soon as your team figures out the answer, yell it out. The first team to get the correct number wins.**

Kids will most likely quickly assume that forty-nine handshakes took place.
However, because handshakes can't be duplicated, only twenty-one took place.

After a team has called out the correct answer, have kids form one big group.

Say: **When I say "go," the members of the winning team should
shake hands with everyone in the room; again, don't repeat any**

LEADER TIP

To calculate the correct answer, figure out how many kids are in the group *minus* the seven winning team members. Multiply that number times seven, and then add twenty-one. For example, if there are fourteen kids in your group without the winning team members, multiply fourteen times seven, and add twenty-one. A team of seven kids that shakes hands with their team members plus fourteen other kids will shake hands 119 times.

handshakes. The first person to complete this task and tell me how many hands the winning team shook is the big winner.

After the game, ask:

● **How is this game like sharing your faith?**

Compare the number of handshakes within a team to the number of handshakes outside a team. Discuss the difference kids can make when they share their faith with people outside the youth group.

FIRE MARSHAL

Overview: Kids will cool off in a hurry as they try to drench an opposing team's player while protecting a teammate.

Game Type: Active, outside, water

Group Size: Any

Time Involved: 10 to 20 minutes

Supplies: A water hose connected to a water source and plastic buckets

Preparation: None

Have kids form two teams, and give each team the same number of buckets. Position the two teams apart from each other but near the water hose they'll be sharing to fill their buckets.

Have each team choose a "fire marshal." Explain that the goal of the game is for kids to completely drench the opposing team's fire marshal while protecting their own.

Say: **At my signal, rush to the hose to begin filling your buckets. You'll have to take turns using the hose, and you'll have to work together to figure out a system for filling your buckets, trying to drench the opposing team's fire marshal, and protecting your own fire marshal. Ready? Go!**

Play ends when one fire marshal is completely wet. Let kids take turns being the fire marshal.

FIVE-SECOND GAME

Overview: Kids will stretch their brains to list five things in a category in five seconds.

Game Type: Quiet, suitable for disabled, travel

Group Size: 2 to 10

Time Involved: 2 to 10 minutes

Supplies: A watch

Preparation: None

Have kids form pairs.

Say: **The object of this game is to stump your partner. The first player will challenge the partner by naming a category—"Name five disciples,"** for example. **Keep in mind that the first player has to be able to name five things in the category he or she chooses. After the first player names the category, the partner has five seconds in which to answer—"Peter, Matthew, James, John, and Thomas,"** for example. **If the partner answers in time, he or she gets a point and gains control of the game. If the partner doesn't answer in time, the first player receives one point and keeps control of the game. However, the partner may also demand that the first player name five things in the category. If the first player can't, then the partner gets a point and gains control of the game. If the first player can, he or she receives two points and keeps control of the game.**

FLIP AND SWITCH

Overview: Kids will use Checkers-type strategy to transform a sentence.

Game Type: Suitable for disabled

Group Size: 10 to 20

Time Involved: 10 to 20 minutes

Supplies: Eight squares of construction paper or carpet, markers, and poster board

Preparation: Lay the squares in a straight line, about two feet apart, leaving a middle square blank. Cut poster board into eight equal pieces. On each piece, write one of the following words: "ever," "faithful," "always," "true," "John," "is," "my," and "friend."

Select eight people to stand on eight squares, leaving the center square open. Give each player one of the following words, on poster board:

Ever faithful always true, (empty square) **John is my friend.**

Have them stand in order from left to right, facing the empty square. Then explain that kids need to achieve the following order:

John is my friend, (empty square) **ever faithful always true.**

Tell kids they must achieve this new order by
● moving forward only,
● moving one space at a time (though they can "jump" one occupied square at a time),
● never passing more than one teammate in a single move, and
● moving so only one person ends up on a square.
Encourage the kids not standing on the bases to help. When no one can move but the sentence hasn't been transformed, all players must return to their original positions.

Here is one possible solution:

"True" moves forward to the open base.

"John" moves around "true" to the open base.

"Is" moves forward to the open base.

"True" moves around "is" to the open base.

"Always" moves around "John."

"Faithful" moves forward to the open base.

"John" moves around "faithful."

"Is" moves around "always."

"My" moves around "true."

"Friend" moves forward to the open base.

"True" moves around "friend."

"Always" moves around "my."

"Faithful" moves around "is."

"Ever" moves around "John."

"John" moves forward.

"Is" moves around "ever."

"My" moves around "faithful."

"Friend" moves around "always."

"Always" moves forward.

"Faithful" moves around "friend."

"Ever" moves around "my."

"My" moves forward.

"Friend" moves around "ever."

"Ever" moves forward.

FOLDER GAME

Overview: Kids will answer trivia questions from folders.

Game Type: Quiet, suitable for disabled

Group Size: 10 to 20

Time Involved: 10 to 20 minutes

Supplies: Folders as described in the "Preparation" section, pencils, paper, and a watch

Preparation: This game requires considerable up-front preparation to make the folders, but you can use the folders again and again. Use plain folders and magazines and newspapers to create categories of trivia questions. For example, label a folder "Advertising." Then cut out twenty advertising slogans or emblems from magazines, and glue them inside the folder. Write a number next to each item; then create an answer key, indicating the company that uses each slogan or emblem.

You could make a "Music" folder with pictures of twenty music stars and groups; a "People in the News" folder with pictures of politicians, well-known business executives, and movie stars; a "Sports" folder with multiple-choice questions about sports rules and heroes; a "History" folder with questions about history; and so on. Just be sure to create an answer key for each folder.

Have kids form teams of three or four. Have the teams find a place in the room where other teams can't hear them well, and then distribute paper and pencils.

Give each team a folder, but tell teams not to look in the folders yet. Have teams label their papers to match the titles on the folders. Explain that teams will have three minutes to answer the questions in a folder.

Start the game. At three minutes, call time. Then have each team pass the folder to another team, and begin the game again.

When each team has seen all the folders, gather everyone together. Go through the answers, and have teams award themselves a point for each correct answer. The team with the most points wins.

FUND-RAISING FOLLIES

Overview: Kids will evaluate fund-raising ideas through friendly, thought-provoking debate.

Game Type: Quiet, senior high, service, suitable for disabled

Group Size: 10 to 20

Time Involved: 30 to 45 minutes

Supplies: Paper, pens, and a watch

Preparation: None

Ask kids to brainstorm for different fund-raising ideas, and write down their ideas on paper. Have kids form teams of five; then explain that they're going to play a debating game to evaluate which fund-raisers might really work.

Say: **I'll name one fund-raising idea, and the first team whose members all stand with their hands raised gets to support that idea. To support an idea, you must figure out how that fund-raiser can be the most successful, keeping in mind the time and cost involved, the resources needed and available, the people needed and available, and so on.**

The other teams must question the fund-raising idea, creating a list of questions, concerns, and challenges to that fund-raiser's success. You'll have five minutes to prepare, and then we'll have a debate. The supporting team will state their ideas, and then the questioning teams must each issue two questions or concerns about the fund-raiser that the supporting team didn't address. Then the supporting team will have two minutes to address those concerns. The questioning teams will have one more chance to ask about loose ends, and the supporting team will have one more chance to address those loose ends.

Keep in mind that the purpose of the game is not to play devil's advocate, but to truly evaluate the fund-raisers.

Start the game by naming one of the fund-raising ideas. Keep time as teams play, and be sure each team gets a chance to support an idea.

FUNNEL HEADS

Overview: Kids will make and use paper funnels to challenge a law of physics.

Game Type: Funny, quiet, suitable for disabled

Group Size: Any

Time Involved: 2 to 10 minutes

Supplies: Paper, tape, and Ping-Pong balls

Preparation: None

Explain to kids that you want them to each blow a Ping-Pong ball out of a funnel. Most kids will think it'll be a cinch.

Distribute paper and tape, and have kids each roll and tape a sheet of paper into a cone or funnel shape. The paper funnels should be large at one end and about one-quarter inch at the other end. (Small kitchen funnels work also if you have access to enough of them.)

Distribute the Ping-Pong balls, and tell the kids to tilt their heads back and hold the funnels in their mouths. Then have kids drop the Ping-Pong balls into their funnels and try to blow the balls out of the funnels by blowing hard and steadily.

To their amazement and consternation, kids won't be able to displace the Ping-Pong balls. After kids have tried for several moments, explain that there's a scientific reason why they couldn't accomplish the task.

Say: **The passage of air actually passes around the ball instead of pushing it upward. So the ball jumps and bounces within the funnel, but it won't bounce out of the funnel.**

GENESIS COUNTDOWN

Overview: Kids will quickly look up Bible verses to answer a unique math problem.

Game Type: Bible, knowledge-builder, quiet, suitable for disabled

Group Size: Any

Time Involved: 2 to 10 minutes

Supplies: Bibles, pencils, and the "Genesis Countdown" handout (p. 37).

Preparation: Make photocopies of the "Genesis Countdown" handout (p. 37).

Have kids form teams of two, and give each team Bibles and a photocopy of the "Genesis Countdown" handout (p. 37).

Say: **When I say "go," begin working on your handouts. We'll see who can figure out this math problem the quickest. Ready? Go!**

When everyone has completed the handout, ask a volunteer to share the answers:

1. 600	6. 127
2. 40	7. 7
3. 350	8. 147
4. 75	9. 12
5. 86	10. 110
	Total: 1,554

VARIATION

If you wish to energize the game even more, assign one member of each team to go to a different room and look up the first Bible passage there. After finding an answer, he or she will run back to the other team member, who will write the answer on the handout. Team members can then switch roles.

Genesis Countdown

1. How old was Noah when the rains came (Genesis 7:11)? _____

2. For how many days did the flood continue to rise (Genesis 7:17)? _____

3. How many years did Noah live after the flood (Genesis 9:28)? _____

4. How old was Abram when he left Haran (Genesis 12:4)? _____

5. How old was Abram when Hagar gave birth to Ishmael (Genesis 16:16)? _____

6. How old was Sarah when she died (Genesis 23:1)? _____

7. How many years of famine did Joseph predict (Genesis 41:30)? _____

8. How old was Jacob when he died (Genesis 47:28)? _____

9. How many tribes of Israel were there (Genesis 49:28)? _____

10. How old was Joseph when he died (Genesis 50:22)? _____

Now add the numbers together: _____

GRACE

Overview: Kids will figure out a riddle to learn about getting all the facts straight.

Game Type: Discussion-starter, no supplies and no preparation, suitable for disabled

Group Size: 2 to 10

Time Involved: 10 to 20 minutes

Supplies: None

Preparation: None

Have kids form teams of four.

Say: **Tonight we have a mystery to solve. A while ago, a robbery was committed. The robber was brought to trial and was convicted, due largely to the testimony of one witness. The jury recommended that the court show grace, even though the robber was found guilty. The judge fined the robber, and the robber never set foot in jail. Why? Your group must solve this riddle.**

LEADER TIP

This game is a good introduction to a discussion on consequences and grace.

After ten to fifteen minutes, ask kids if they've arrived at an answer or if they're ready for you to tell them the situation. If you need to, explain that the robber and the eyewitness were Siamese twins. The court could not punish the guilty robber without also punishing the innocent brother.

GRID TICK-TACK-TOE

Overview: Kids will play Tick-Tack-Toe with a twist.

Game Type: Quiet, suitable for disabled

Group Size: Any

Time Involved: 2 to 10 minutes

Supplies: Paper and pencils

Preparation: None

Have kids form pairs, and give each pair a sheet of paper and two pencils. Have each pair draw a tick-tack-toe grid and then draw lines to close the grid in, forming nine squares. Instead of placing an X or an O in the square, partners will place their marks on each line intersection.

Have each pair determine who will place which mark. Even though there are now sixteen choices in which to place the mark, it still requires three in a row to win.

> ## VARIATION
>
> You can turn this into a tournament by having the winners of each round progress to play each other at a different table.

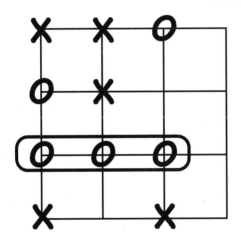

GUESSWORK

Overview: Kids will work together to sharpen their estimating skills.

Game Type: Quiet, suitable for disabled, travel

Group Size: Any

Time Involved: 2 to 10 minutes

Supplies: Newspapers, paper, pencils, and scissors

Preparation: None

Have kids form small groups of three or four, and give each group a single page of a newspaper. Tell groups they'll have one minute to estimate how many words are written on their newspaper pages. Have groups appoint a recorder to write down their estimates. After one minute, call time. Ask groups to explain how they arrived at their estimates.

Give each group a pair of scissors, and have group members cut their newspaper page into as many pieces as there are group members. Have each group member count the words in his or her section of the page. Then have kids tally the results and see how close their estimate came to the actual number of words.

> ## VARIATION
>
> Play this game using other estimates, such as how many books are in the church library or how many kernels are in a bag of popcorn.

HYMNS AND HUMMINGS

Overview: Kids will write lyrics to hymns, based on the hymns' titles.

Game Type: Musical, suitable for disabled

Group Size: 2 to 10

Time Involved: 10 to 20 minutes

Supplies: Hymnals, paper, and pens

Preparation: Select a variety of hymns with interesting titles from the hymnal. Write down the title of each hymn on a different piece of paper.

Have kids form pairs. Distribute a pen and a sheet of paper with a hymn title to each pair. Tell the teenagers to use the title as a guideline for writing lyrics for a song. Encourage the kids to be creative and to write lyrics that are personally meaningful.

Give kids a few minutes to write lyrics. When kids have finished, ask each pair to read the title of their song and sing or read the lyrics they've written. Then have the pair read aloud the actual lyrics from a hymnal.

I Can Play the Stick Game

Overview: Kids will try to figure out how to play the stick game.

Game Type: Junior high, quiet, suitable for disabled

Group Size: Any

Time Involved: 2 to 10 minutes

Supplies: A broom handle or other large stick

Preparation: None

Have kids form a circle and sit down. Explain that you'll start the game but the kids will have to figure out how to play the game.

Hold up the stick and say: **OK, I can play the stick game. Can you play the stick game?**

LEADER TIP

To further confuse the kids, speak in an unusual manner, accentuating certain words. Also, pass the stick in a random manner.

Then hand the stick to someone else, who will attempt to play the game by duplicating what you've done. To play correctly, the person must say "OK" before saying, "I can play the stick game. Can you play the stick game?" If the person plays correctly, ask him or her to pass the stick to another person. If the person doesn't play correctly, take the stick back, and hand it to someone else. Play until everyone has deciphered the secret rule.

I Won't Eat Camel Burgers!

Overview: Kids will attempt to solve a riddle based on an inheritance battle.

Game Type: Quiet, suitable for disabled, travel

Group Size: Any

Time Involved: 2 to 10

Supplies: Pencils and paper

Preparation: None

Have kids form groups of four, and distribute paper and pencils to each group. Read the following story to the group:

> Many years ago, a wealthy Israelite issued a decree that detailed how he wished his estate to be divided. The most significant of his possessions was a small herd of camels that had been left to him by his father. There were now only seventeen left. His allotted to his eldest son half of the camels, to his second son, one-third of the camels, and to his youngest son, one-ninth of the camels. Indicate that these fractions don't add up.
>
> Since the brothers weren't hungry for camel burgers, they asked the advice of their wealthy uncle, who owned the other portion of Granddad's camel herd. The uncle proposed a workable solution.
>
> In your group of three brothers and an uncle, try to figure out the solution the uncle proposed—and it didn't require ketchup or buns. Encourage your kids to think creatively.

Here is one solution: The uncle loaned the boys one camel (on paper, of course) so the brothers were able to perform the mathematical calculations. The brothers calculated that half of eighteen is nine, one-third of eighteen is six, and one-ninth of eighteen is two. Nine plus six plus two equal seventeen, so the brothers were able to return the loaned camel before he ever hit the sand!

IF ONLY YOU'D BEEN PAYING ATTENTION

Overview: Kids will choose definitions of words.

Game Type: Knowledge-builder, quiet, suitable for disabled, travel

Group Size: Any

Time Involved: 10 to 20 minutes

Supplies: A watch

Preparation: None

Have kids form trios, and then announce that they'll be playing a word game they can win easily if they've paid attention in school. Explain that you'll read aloud a word with three possible definitions and then ask the trios to choose the correct definition.

But there's a catch: Trio members will have twenty seconds to reach a consensus and choose a definition. Then they must cast a vote.

Here are a dozen words and definitions to share (based on Webster's New World College Dictionary). The correct definition is italicized. Additional words are readily available in your dictionary!

Oxbow
Parts of an ox yoke
A knot used to tie a bow tie
A medieval stringed instrument

Pinole
A game popular among children in Central America
Italian embroidery
Flour made from ground corn

Pruritus
Itching of the skin
Latin for "distant port"
The cloak worn by a Russian Orthodox priest

Scrivener
A puzzle enthusiast
A scribe or clerk
The connecting rod between two gears on a turbine engine

Adenoma
A benign tumor of glandular origin
A star system
The symbol used to represent "and"

Malfeasance
A soft-shelled mollusk found in the Atlantic Ocean
A sickness that causes boils and blisters
Wrongdoing by a public official

Balas
A woven rope used by Argentine cowboys
A port town in Bolivia
A semiprecious stone

Legerdemain
Sleight of hand
Shirt traditionally worn with lederhosen
The dorsal fin of a blue tuna

Inimical
To inhale
Like an enemy
Bottling or canning liquids

Gegenschein
Fine German lace
A diffuse, faint light
A subproton, discovered prior to the quark and after the atom

Fardel
Gossip
A butterfly's membranous wings
A pack, burden, or misfortune

Discalced
A degenerative bone disease
Term for a cleaned printing press
Barefooted

IMPROVISATION CREATION

Overview: Kids will scramble to improvise skits.

Game Type: Funny, suitable for disabled

Group Size: 20 to 30

Time Involved: 20 to 30 minutes

Supplies: Paper, a pencil, and a watch

Preparation: None

Have kids gather around you.

Say: **I'd like you to call out a bunch of words—just the first words that come to mind.**

Write down the words kids call out, especially the verbs, nouns, adjectives, and adverbs. Then have kids form groups of five.

Say: **Now you're going to participate in a type of acting called improvisation. I'll give each group five words. You'll have two minutes to prepare, and then you'll perform a skit for us! One or more of the words** can be your title, the name of a character, part of the dialogue, or whatever you want. Your skit must be two minutes long, so you'll have to work together to keep the skit going without planned lines or action.

VARIATION If you have a particularly dramatic group, call out words during the improvisation so the actors improvise as they're acting.

When everyone understands, select five words from your list for the first group, five words for the second group, and so on. After two minutes, call the groups back together. Have the groups perform their skits, and time each group to make sure the skit lasts two minutes. Afterward, applaud the kids' efforts; then have them form new groups and improvise again.

INFINITE AFFINITIES

Overview: Kids will race against the clock to complete word pairs.

Game Type: Quiet, suitable for disabled, travel

Group Size: 10 to 20

Time Involved: 2 to 10 minutes

Supplies: A watch, paper, and pencil

Preparation: Prepare a list of affinities. Avoid listing the affinities in any order, such as alphabetical or topical. You may use the "Infinite Affinities" handout (p. 46-47) or create your own.

Have kids form three or four teams. Explain that affinities are familiar expressions that usually include the word "and"—"night and day," for example. Tell kids that you'll read aloud an unfinished affinity to one team, and then that team has five seconds to shout out the correct completion. Add that the missing word will be represented by its number of letters. For example, you'll say, "night and three" for "night and day."

Say: **Each team will begin the game with ten points, and a wrong answer or a blank will cost you one point.**

Start the game with the first team. If a team fails to say the correct word within five seconds, announce the correct word, and then *immediately* proceed to the next team. Repeat the process, team-by-team in rapid succession, until only one team has points left.

Infinite Affinities

Adam and 3 (Eve)

Rod and 4 (Reel)

Hat and 4 (Coat)

Naughty and 4 (Nice)

Cain and 4 (Abel)

Abbott and 8 (Costello)

Thunder and 9 (Lightning)

Touch and 2 (Go)

Sugar and 5 (Spice)

Open and 4 (Shut)

Part and 6 (Parcel)

Assault and 7 (Battery)

Cup and 6 (Saucer)

Cap and 4 (Gown)

Bow and 5 (Arrow)

Heaven and 4 (Hell)

Jack and 4 (Jill)

David and 7 (Goliath)

Give and 4 (Take)

Right and 5 (Wrong)

Ice and 4 (Snow)

Army and 4 (Navy)

Bread and 6 (Butter)

Bait and 6 (Switch)

Checks and 8 (Balances)

Liver and 6 (Onions)

Hugs and 6 (Kisses)

In and 3 (Out)

Hit and 3 (Run)

Horse and 5 (Wagon)

Spit and 6 (Polish)

Tweedledee and 7-3 (Tweedledum)

Gas and 3 (Oil)

Mom and 3 (Dad)

Hammer and 4 (Nail)

Ice Cream and 4 (Cake)

Cats and 4 (Dogs)

Heaven and 5 (Earth)

Rock and 4 (Roll)

Shoes and 5 (Socks)

Salt and 6 (Pepper)

Soap and 5 (Water)

Tried and 4 (True)

Half and 4 (Half)

Cheese and 8 (Crackers)

Night and 3 (Day)

House and 3 (Lot)

Gold and 6 (Silver)

Rise and 4 (Fall)

Smoke and 7 (Mirrors)

Stars and 7 (Stripes)

The Just and 3-6 (The Unjust)

Widows and 7 (Orphans)

North and 5 (South)

Ebb and 4 (Flow)

Samson and 7 (Delilah)

Comb and 5 (Brush)

Death and 5 (Taxes)

Prayer and 10 (Meditation)

Wholesale and 6 (Retail)

Stocks and 5 (Bonds)

Saddle and 6 (Bridle)

Bits and 6 (Pieces)

Pharisees and 9 (Sadducees)

Spaghetti and 9 (Meatballs)

Come and 2 (Go)

Down and 3 (Out)

Meat and 8 (Potatoes)

Good and 3 (Bad)

Flint and 5 (Steel)

Ham and 4 (Eggs)

Sodom and 8 (Gomorrah)

Brush and 4 (Comb)

Bed and 9 (Breakfast)

Fine and 5 (Dandy)

Needle and 6 (Thread)

East and 4 (West)

Fire and 3 (Ice)

Nuts and 5 (Bolts)

Law and 5 (Order)

Alpha and 5 (Omega)

Room and 5 (Board)

Pork and 5 (Beans)

Lock and 3 (Key)

Macaroni and 6 (Cheese)

War and 5 (Peace)

Pen and 3 (Ink)

Stand and 7 (Deliver)

Jews and 8 (Gentiles)

Refuge and 8 (Strength)

Life and 5 (Death)

Forgive and 6 (Forget)

Prim and 6 (Proper)

Flesh and 5 (Blood)

Lord and 6 (Savior)

Fire and 9 (Brimstone)

Lad and 6 (Lassie)

Huff and 4 (Puff)

Trial and 5 (Error)

Well and 4 (Good)

Weep and 4 (Wail)

Pro and 3 (Con)

Boom and 4 (Bust)

Bulls and 5 (Bears)

Book and 4 (Page)

Tea and 8 (Crumpets)

Nip and 4 (Tuck)

Above and 6 (Beyond)

Cut and 5 (Paste)

Wild and 6 (Woolly)

First and 8 (Foremost)

Loaves and 6 (Fishes)

Father and 3 (Son)

Trials and 12 (Tribulations)

Get Up and 2 (Go)

INFLATO!

Overview: Kids will attempt to inflate three plastic trash bags, each time increasing their speed.

Game Type: Active, discussion-starter, suitable for disabled

Group Size: Any

Time Involved: 2 to 10 minutes

Supplies: Paper, several large plastic trash bags, and a watch

Preparation: None

Have kids sit in a circle, and give each person a sheet of paper to roll into a tube. Explain that you'll pass a plastic trash bag around the circle and that each player is to try to blow through a paper tube to fill the bag.

Say: **When you're finished with the bag, pass it to the next person. We'll see how long it takes us to fill the bag.**

Start the bag around, and time the group. When the bag returns to you, tie the open end into a knot. Then repeat the activity two more times with other trash bags. Encourage kids to find new ways to inflate the bags and improve their time. Afterward, ask:

- **Was it possible to fill the three bags with air equally? Why or why not?**
- **What might this teach us about endurance?**

Say: **No matter how well prepared we are, each of us will eventually "give out" unless we learn to pace ourselves.**

IT'S A POTSHOT

Overview: Kids will try to move a pot of water using only ropes.

Game Type: Outside, suitable for disabled

Group Size: 20 to 30

Time Involved: 30 to 45 minutes

Supplies: A round pot full of water, string, and a fairly long piece of sturdy rope

Preparation: Use string to make a circle boundary, and place the pot full of water in the middle.

Have kids form teams of four to six. Explain that teams will try to pick up the pot full of water and move it outside the circle.

Say: **The catch is that you can't touch the pot with any part of your body and you must use a rope to move the pot outside the circle.**

Tell teams they'll be allowed one chance until all the teams have tried. If they spill the water, touch the pot, or fail to move the pot, the next team will get a chance.

Allow teams to strategize for a few minutes, and then ask a team to volunteer to go first. Allow each group to try, but be prepared to show kids the solution in case you need to.

LEADER TIP

It's a good idea to practice the solution so you can demonstrate how to move the pot of water if the teams aren't able to.

Here's a solution: Fold the rope over once. Then place the rope around the pot so you have two equal lengths of rope on either side of the pot. Ask a volunteer to help you twist the ends of the rope in opposite directions. The rope will become tight enough so you can pick up the pot and carry it outside the circle.

KNOT!

Overview: Kids will learn new skills as they try "knot" to lose a race.

Game Type: Knowledge-builder, quiet, suitable for disabled

Group Size: Any

Time Involved: 10 to 20 minutes

Supplies: A three-foot length of rope or cord for every two teenagers and the "Knotty Problems" handout (p. 51).

Preparation: Make photocopies of the "Knotty Problems" handout (p. 51).

Have kids form two teams, and then have team members form pairs. Each team should have the same number of pairs. If you have an uneven number of kids on a team, let that team include a trio.

Give each pair a length of rope and a copy of the "Knotty Problems" handout (p. 51). Assign each pair one of the six knots on the handout. If you have more than six pairs on a team, it's OK to assign a knot more than once. If you have fewer than six pairs, just assign as many knots as you have pairs. Explain that some of the knots call for looping the rope around a post or ring, so kids can simply turn a chair over and use one of the upturned legs as a post.

The object of the game is to see how quickly pairs can learn to tie the knots correctly. The first team to complete its knots correctly will be the winner. Since knot-tying may be unfamiliar to your kids, caution teams to keep tying, even if another team seems to be finished. There's a good chance some of the team's knots may be incorrect. If a knot is tied incorrectly, the pair must untie it and begin again.

Incorporate friend-making skills by encouraging pairs to help each other figure out their knots. This game can be played again and again simply by assigning different knots to different pairs.

Knotty Problems

1. Use an **overhand knot** to put a knot in the end of a rope.
2. Make a **half hitch** to fasten the end of a rope after it's been looped over a post.
3. Use a **clove hitch** to tie one end of a rope around a tree.
4. Make a **sheepshank** to shorten a rope without cutting it.
5. Use a **bowline** to make a loop that won't slip.
6. Use a **taut line hitch** to make a loop that will slide.

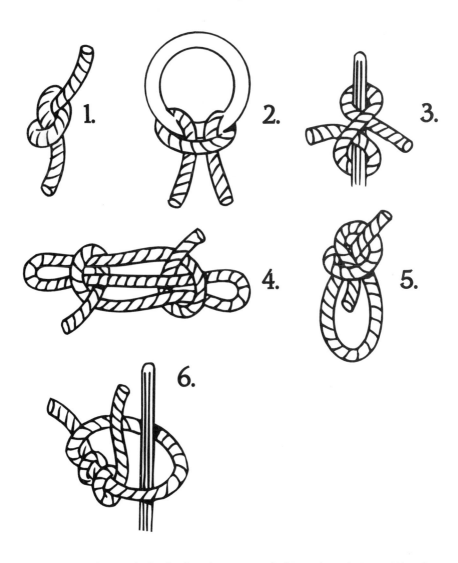

LABELS

Overview: Kids will guess food products from ingredient lists.

Game Type: Funny, quiet, suitable for disabled

Group Size: 2 to 10

Time Involved: 2 to 10 minutes

Supplies: A paper bag and labels from cans or boxes of food, especially food with strange ingredients, such as hot dogs, snack cakes, specialty canned foods, boxed cereals, dairy products, and frozen items

Preparation: Place the labels or food items in a paper bag so kids won't be able to see them.

Read aloud each ingredient label, and award a point to the first person to guess the food item.

THE LAST WILL BE FIRST

Overview: Kids will think of Bible words that begin with the letter that another word ended with.

Game Type: Bible, discussion-starter, quiet, suitable for disabled

Group Size: Any

Time Involved: 10 to 20 minutes

Supplies: Bibles and a watch

Preparation: None

Have kids form teams of two or three, and distribute Bibles.

Say: **The object of this word game is to come up with a word from the Bible that begins with the same letter that the previous word ended with. For example, if the first team says "Adam," the next team could say "Mount Sinai." Then the next team could say "Israel." We'll have a twenty-second time limit, and you can look in your Bibles. If you can't come up with a word, your team is out.**

Start the game, and have kids play until only one team is left. Use the game to lead into a discussion about the last being first (Mark 10:31).

LETTER MYSTERIES

Overview: Kids will create letter mysteries, exchange them, and solve them.

Game Type: Affirmation, quiet, suitable for disabled

Group Size: Any

Time Involved: 10 to 20 minutes

Supplies: Paper, tape, and pencils

Preparation: Write down a couple of letter mysteries as examples for kids. For example, you could write down the following letter mysteries:

**MAN
BOARD**

1. (answer: man overboard)

Seeingseeing

2. (answer: seeing double)

Explain to kids that letter mysteries are words arranged to communicate a different word or concept. Show the kids the examples you wrote down before class. Then have kids each create a letter mystery that expresses what the group means to them or relates to what you're studying. Suggest that kids first jot down words and experiences that come to mind when they think about the group and then create a "picture" from those words. For example, "A hug in hard times" could become "haHrdUtimGes."

Give kids several minutes to create their letter mysteries and tape them to a wall. Then challenge everyone to figure out the solutions to each letter mystery.

LIARS AND TRUTH-TELLERS

Overview: Kids will decipher if they're being told a lie or the truth.

Game Type: Discussion-starter, junior high, quiet, suitable for disabled

Group Size: Any

Time Involved: 2 to 10 minutes

Supplies: None

Preparation: Call two teenagers before the game, and ask for their help. Ask one person to play the part of the liar who can't tell the truth. Ask the other person to play the part of the truth-teller who can't lie. Explain to both that during the game you'll ask them if they're liars. The liar should say, "No, but the next person is because he (or she) admitted it to me." The truth-teller should simply say, "No, I certainly am not."

Have the two volunteers wait in another room while you tell the rest of the group the following story:

> In the mythical town of Knowledgeville, there are only liars and truth-tellers. The liars can tell only lies, and the truth-tellers can tell only the truth. We happen to have two of their citizens with us tonight. I am going to bring them in one at a time and ask them each one question. It will be your job to determine if each person is lying or telling the truth.

Bring in the liar, and ask if he or she is a liar. After the response, bring in the truth-teller, and repeat the process. Then ask the liar and the truth-teller to leave so their facial expressions don't give them away. Have the other kids form groups of three or four and determine whether your volunteers were liars or truth-tellers. After a few minutes of discussion, have groups offer answers.

If kids get stuck, remind kids that the first person said the second person admitted to being a liar. If the second person were a liar, he or she couldn't admit to being a liar because that would be the truth. That means the first person is a liar and the second person is a truth-teller.

Continue with a discussion on how subtle lying and deceitfulness can be.

LIVING ALPHABET

Overview: Kids will be speedy spellers in this fast-paced game.

Game Type: Active, funny, outside

Group Size: More than 75

Time Involved: 20 to 30 minutes

Supplies: Cardboard or poster board squares and a marker

Preparation: Write each letter of the alphabet on a separate piece of cardboard. You'll need four complete alphabets.

Have kids form four teams, and have each team choose a captain. Have captains distribute the alphabet letters to their teams. If you have a large group, each team member can have a letter. If you have a smaller group, each team member can have several letters.

Have teams line up facing each other. Allow about four feet between lines. Members of each team should be arranged alphabetically. (If kids have multiple letters, have them place their letters on the ground in front of them.)

When you call out a word to spell, team members with the appropriate letters will rush out and try to spell the word by holding the letters up facing their opponents. In the excitement, they are likely to assume wrong positions. The captains must make sure their teammates are arranged in the proper order. The game leader decides which team first correctly spelled the word.

Where a double letter occurs, the player holding that letter should swing the letter back and forth. Where a letter appears in more than one place in the words, that player should run from place to place in the word holding up the letter until a winner is announced.

> ## VARIATION
>
> To make the game more challenging or to tie it to your studies, call out questions on the Bible, history, geography, or famous people, and have teams spell out the answers.

MAKE THE MOST OF IT

Overview: Kids will list items in a variety of categories.

Game Type: Quiet, suitable for disabled

Group Size: Any

Time Involved: 20 to 30 minutes

Supplies: Paper, pencils, and a watch

Preparation: None

Have kids form small teams of three or four, depending on your class size. Give each team a pencil and a supply of paper. Have each team choose someone to be the recorder.

Tell teams you'll call out a category and then they'll have three minutes to write down as many items as they can think of that fit in the category. The group with the longest list wins. Use the following categories, or think of others yourself.

- automobile models
- tree varieties
- vegetables
- sports teams
- Italian foods

VARIATION

For an extra challenge, tell kids their answers have to begin with a certain letter of the alphabet.

For the next round, have groups exercise their imaginations by making lists that fit the following categories. You may want to increase the time allowed to five minutes.

- new uses for tires
- new subjects to take in school
- new uses for paper bags
- new inventions you'd like to see

For the final installment of the game, have kids test their brain power by thinking of as many solutions to the following problems as possible.

- Someone just delivered twenty-five live turkeys to your door.
- You found a canvas gym bag full of money.
- You're stuck in a blizzard, and the only things in your refrigerator are ten oranges and a loaf of bread.
- You're in a daze and wear your little brother's pants and mismatched shoes to school by mistake. The principal asks you to address the student body during an assembly.

Man-iac Words

Overview: Kids will list words that contain smaller words.

Game Type: No supplies and no preparation, quiet, suitable for disabled, travel

Group Size: 2 to 10

Time Involved: 2 to 10 minutes

Supplies: None

Preparation: None

Choose a short word or letter combination, such as "man." Explain that each person should think of a word that encompasses the smaller word. Add that each player's larger word must be different from the other players' words.

For example, if you say "man," players could say the following words: **man**ager, **man**iac, **man**hole, police**man**, **man**gy, **man**dolin, **man**ger, **Man**hattan, **man**ifold, Sa**man**tha, e**man**cipate, and so on.

Start the game with a selected player, and move it clockwise around the room. If a player draws a blank, he or she may pass. Continue until everyone has to pass.

Map Attack

Overview: Kids will draw maps based solely on verbal descriptions from teammates.

Game Type: Funny, knowledge-builder, senior high, suitable for disabled

Group Size: 10 to 20

Time Involved: 20 to 30 minutes

Supplies: A chalkboard, chalk, a map of your town, paper, pen, scissors, and a hat or bag

Preparation: Make a list of several locations in your town; include some out-of-the-way places or strange landmarks. Also mark the locations on the town map. For example, you might list youth hot spots, athletic or concert arenas, laundry or dry-cleaning establishments, rural sights, historical markers, and vacant lots. Cut apart the list so each location is on a separate slip of paper, and put the slips into the hat.

Have kids form teams of five. Explain that kids will take turns drawing detailed maps on the chalkboard as their teammates describe the locations of various places.

Have the first person from the first team approach the chalkboard, and have a team member draw a location from the hat. Have the team members tell the person at the chalkboard how to draw a map to that location. However, no one may say the name of any location aloud. Team members may only mention the names of roads and the directions north, south, east, and west.

Allow two minutes for each attempt. Compare the drawing with the actual city map for some funny results.

MISSING-OBJECT GAME

Overview: Kids will attempt to figure out which items are missing from a pile.

Game Type: Quiet, suitable for disabled

Group Size: Any

Time Involved: 10 to 20 minutes

Supplies: A bag and a variety of objects with which to make a pile

Preparation: Pile the objects on a table so kids will be able to see each item.

Have kids study the pile for a few minutes. Then ask a volunteer to turn off the lights. Place a few objects in the bag. Ask the volunteer to turn on the lights again. Then ask kids to name what items are missing. The people who name the most missing items win the game. Play several rounds.

Mission Impossible

Overview: Kids will try to steal a set of keys from a blindfolded group member.

Game Type: Funny, quiet

Group Size: Any

Time Involved: 10 to 20 minutes

Supplies: Key chain with a bunch of noisy keys and a blindfold

Preparation: None

Have everyone sit in a circle. Ask for a volunteer to sit in the middle of the circle; blindfold the volunteer. Place the set of keys on the floor directly in front of the blindfolded person. Explain that you will walk around the outside of the circle and tap people on the head.

Say: **If I tap you, you have to try to sneak into the middle of the circle, grab the keys, and return to the outside of the circle without getting caught. Everyone must be absolutely silent. The blindfolded person will point with an index finger and say "gotcha" to try to "catch" the thieves. If the blindfolded person points at you, you're caught and must collapse in place. But other thieves may use collapsed bodies as blockades to avoid getting caught themselves.**

LEADER TIP

Keep the game moving by sending more than one person at a time to steal the keys. Also be sure kids understand that you're the final authority as to whether or not a thief was caught.

Also explain that the blindfolded person may say "gotcha" only once per second instead of pointing in rapid-fire succession.

If a person successfully steals the keys and returns to the outside of the circle, he or she becomes the blindfolded person in the middle of the circle.

MIXED MESSAGES

Overview: Kids will try to communicate without phones, computers, or even voices!

Game Type: Knowledge-builder, night, outside, suitable for disabled

Group Size: Any

Time Involved: 20 to 30 minutes

Supplies: Flashlights or whistles, paper, pens, and the "Mixed Messages" handout (p. 61)

Preparation: Photocopy the "Mixed Messages" handout (p. 61).

Have kids form groups of at least four. Groups will signal to each other in this game, so be sure kids form an even number of groups. Have groups number off; then explain that even-numbered groups will signal to each other, as will odd-numbered groups.

Give each player a copy of the "Mixed Messages" handout (p. 61), and give each group a supply of paper and pens. If you play in the daylight, give each group a whistle. If you play at night, give each group two flashlights, one to signal with and another to decipher the codes with.

Have kids study the handout. Then demonstrate signaling a few words, and let kids practice deciphering as a large group. You might want to start with something really simple, such as "cat" or "dog" or your name. Then go over the basic signaling instructions at the bottom of the handout.

When you think kids are ready, have groups spread out and think of a word to signal to their partner groups. If you're going to play outside at night, let kids do their brainstorming indoors first. Tell kids to make sure someone writes down what they see and hear from the other group so kids can then turn to the handout to decipher the message.

Have groups stand across from each other in a large open area. If you have more than two groups, make sure there's enough distance between sets of groups so messages don't become confused. Then stand back and let the messages begin!

It may take a while for kids to get the hang of the system, but with practice, messages can become more and more involved.

MiXeD MessaGes

Morse code is an international system for sending messages by using dots and dashes. Here are the basics.

International Morse Code

A •–	G – – •	N – •	U • • –
B – • • •	H • • • •	O – – –	V • • • –
C – • – •	I • •	P • – – •	W • – –
D – • •	J • – – –	Q – – • –	X – • • –
E •	K – • –	R • – •	Y – • – –
F • • – •	L • – • •	S • • •	Z – – • •
	M – –	T –	

Technique

Here's how to signal with a flashlight or a whistle.

	Flashlight	Whistle
Dot	Short flash	Short blast
Dash	Long flash	Long blast
End of Letter	Short darkness (count 1)	Short silence (count 1)
End of Word	Long darkness (count 1-2-3)	Long silence (count 1-2-3)

Basic Signaling Instructions

- Signal all dots and dashes for one letter without stopping.
- To get attention, send four A's (•–•–•–•–) without stopping.
- Signal IMI (• •– –• •) when you want someone to repeat a message.
- Signal T (-) when you understand the message.
- To erase a mistake, signal eight E's (• • • • • • • •), then signal the word correctly.
- To show that your message is complete, signal AR (•–•–•).

MOSQUITO MADNESS

Overview: Kids will try to figure out which two students are the "mosquitoes"—before they get "bit"!

Game Type: Quiet, suitable for disabled

Group Size: 20 to 30

Time Involved: 20 to 30 minutes

Supplies: A deck of cards

Preparation: None

LEADER TIP

If you have a small group (ten to twenty students), you can play this game using one jack and one ace. If you have a large group (more than forty students), you can play this game using more than two jacks and more than two aces.

Have kids form a circle. Count out a card for each person, making sure you include two jacks and two aces. Deal one card to each person, and instruct kids not to show their cards to anyone. Then explain that the two people who received jacks will be the "mosquitoes," the two people who received aces will be the "exterminators," and everyone else will be people.

Tell the kids that the game will begin with everyone pretending to take a nap with head down and eyes closed.

Say: **Then I'll ask the mosquitoes to open their eyes and raise their heads. The mosquitoes will quietly use hand motions to decide who they've "bitten." Mosquitoes, you'll have to be quiet because you don't want to give yourselves away. The mosquitoes will put their heads down again, and I'll ask the exterminators to open their eyes and raise their heads. The exterminators will quietly use hand motions to decide who to accuse of being a mosquito. Exterminators, you'll have to be quiet, too, because you don't want to give yourselves away either. After the exterminators put their heads down again, I'll ask you all to open your eyes and look up.**

Explain that you'll then announce who's been bitten by the mosquitoes and that person must show his or her card and sit out of the game. Then you'll announce whether the exterminators chose correctly. Be sure you don't say who the exterminators accused. If the exterminators chose correctly, the mosquito must show his or her card and sit out of the game. If the extermi-nators chose incorrectly, simply continue the game.

Say: **At that point, you will all get to vote on who you think a mos-quito might be. Whether you're correct or not, that person must show his or her card and sit out of the game.**

When everyone understands, have kids play until they figure out who the mosquitoes are or until the mosquitoes are all who remain.

NAME BRIDGES

Overview: Kids will stretch their word power with this vocabulary game.

Game Type: Knowledge-builder, quiet, suitable for disabled

Group Size: Any

Time Involved: 2 to 10 minutes

Supplies: Paper, pencils, and a watch

Preparation: None

Have kids form pairs, and distribute paper and pencils. Have the partners with the longest names write their first names vertically down the left side of the papers and then draw a line from the letter across the page to the right. Then have the second partners write their first names vertically *up* the right side of the paper, lining up the letters with the lines and using letters from a middle or last name if needed. For example, if Elizabeth Brown is playing with Chantel Smith, the paper will look like this:

```
E_____M
L_____S
I_____L
Z_____E
A_____T
BEETHOVE  N
E_____A
T_____H
H_____C
```

Each partner will need a copy of this grid. When everyone has finished making his or her grid, explain that the goal of the game is to write in a word that begins and ends with the letters provided.

Give kids three minutes to fill in their grids. Then have kids count their points as follows: five points for the longest word in each letter combination and one point for each letter used in the entire grid.

Have kids form different pairs and play again. The first player to reach 150 points wins.

Name Game

Overview: Kids will work together to quickly recall names of places, people, and things.

Game Type: Quiet, suitable for disabled

Group Size: Any

Time Involved: 10 to 20 minutes

Supplies: A watch

Preparation: None

Have kids form teams of two or three. Explain that teams will compete against each other for the title of "Supreme Trivia Commandos." Begin by selecting a category: people, places, or things.

Say: **One team will start by naming something or someone in the se-lected category. For example, for the "people" category, the first group might say, "Abraham Lincoln." Then within five seconds the second team must say the name of *another* person whose name begins with the last letter of the person mentioned by the first group. After hearing "Abraham Lincoln," for example, the second team might say "Nero." Then the third team might say, "Oliver Twist." Explain that the first team that can't respond in five seconds will have the opportunity to claim a new category and start a new challenge.**

Start the game by naming a category. As your kids get the idea of the game, consider narrowing the categories to items like "biblical people" or "people in fairy tales."

NAME THAT MORAL

Overview: Kids will deduce morals to Aesop's fables.

Game Type: Discussion-starter, knowledge-builder, quiet, suitable for disabled, travel

Group Size: 2 to 10

Time Involved: 10 to 20 minutes

Supplies: A book of Aesop's fables (readily found in most libraries and used bookstores)

Preparation: None

Have kids form teams of two to three. Read aloud a fable, and ask teenagers to guess the moral to the fable. The team that first guesses the moral correctly can read the next fable to the rest of the group.

LEADER TIP

Use this game to spark conversation among your kids or to introduce a heavier Bible study time. Many fables touch upon biblical themes. For example, "The Lion and the Mouse" teaches about friendship, and "The Ants and the Grasshopper" teaches preparation.

VARIATION

You might also challenge your teenagers to create stories to complement a particular moral. For example, ask kids to create a story to teach the moral "Work in season, and rest later." You could also have kids create stories to teach different proverbs from the Bible.

NEVER-ENDING TRIANGLES

Overview: Kids will try to form triangles one segment at a time.

Game Type: Quiet, suitable for disabled, travel

Group Size: Any

Time Involved: 2 to 10 minutes

Supplies: Paper and pencils

Preparation: None

Have the players form pairs or trios, and distribute paper and pencils. Have each group make a triangle shape on its sheet of paper by starting with five equally spaced dots on the bottom line, then four on the next row, then three dots, then two dots, and then a single dot at the top.

Explain that each player in turn will connect two dots, horizontally or diagonally. The goal is to close a triangle by adding the final line segment. When a player closes a triangle, he or she writes his or her initials inside the triangle. Closing a three-dot triangle is worth one point. Closing a larger triangle is worth two points. The player with the most points when all the line segments have been drawn wins.

<table>
<tr><td>

VARIATION

You can make this game longer and more challenging by increasing the size of the original triangle.

</td></tr>
</table>

Nickel Challenge

Overview: Kids will test their memories about nickels.

Game Type: Discussion-starter, quiet, suitable for disabled, travel

Group Size: Any

Time Involved: 2 to 10 minutes

Supplies: Nickels, paper, and a pen

Preparation: None

Give each teenager a nickel, and direct kids to ask each other quiz questions about things found on that coin. Each person should keep the coin concealed, looking at it after each question is answered to check the accuracy of the answer. Start with the questions below, and then invite kids to add their own.

- Whose head is on the head side?
- What building is on the tail side?
- In what year was your nickel minted?
- What hairstyle is the man wearing?
- What is the phrase motto on the head side?
- What is the single word motto on the head side?
- What is the phrase motto on the tail/building side?
- How many columns are on the building?
- Is the edge of the coin smooth or bumpy?

Point out that we use nickels almost every day but probably haven't noticed these details. The same thing can happen with friends: We either don't take time to know them or don't take time to know the new things that are happening in their lives.

NIGHT HUNT

Overview: Kids will play Hide-and-Seek with a twist.

Game Type: Active, discussion-starter, night, outside, senior high

Group Size: Any

Time Involved: 45 to 60 minutes

Supplies: Paper, pens, tacks, a watch, and flashlights

Preparation: Scout out the area to make sure it's safe. For example, check for poison oak, beehives, and other dangers.

This game is ideal for a retreat or evening camp activity. Explain to the players that they will be playing a game similar to Hide-and-Seek, but with strategy. Have kids form four teams. (If you have more than thirty players, have kids form eight teams, and run two games at the same time.) Separate the teams, and have one volunteer go with each team and explain its role, preventing the other teams from knowing one another's roles. Explain the roles as follows:

- **Hiders** have to find a good hiding place for their entire team.
- **Hunters** have to find the hiders.
- **Hinderers** follow the hiders to their hiding spot and try to think of ways to mislead the hunters—writing notes and tacking them onto surrounding trees or creating barriers using sticks or picnic benches, for example. Remind the hinderers to be clever about it.
- **Helpers** also follow the hiders to their hiding spot, but then think of ways to lead the hunters to them. Helpers can't destroy anything the hinderers write or set up, but they must leave their own clever notes and perhaps design barriers blocking incorrect paths.

Give the hiders about ten minutes to hide, and allow the helpers and hinderers ten minutes to do their work. Then have the hunters look for the hiders. The helpers and hinderers can't follow the hunters, but they can stand on the side and yell hints and clues. Unfortunately for the hunters, they don't know which team is the helpers and which team is the hinderers. Give the hunters a reasonable amount of time to find the hiders.

When the hunters find the hiders or when time runs out, have everyone form a circle in a large open area. Then lead kids into a discussion about the challenges to discovering God's will for our lives. Explain that in this game, the hunters can represent us and the hiders can represent God's will. Ask:

- **Who do you think the helpers and hinderers represent?**

The helpers represent Scripture, God's voice, other Christians, and so on. The hinderers represent Satan at work.

- **What types of tactics did the helpers and hinderers try to use?**
- **Did the helpers or hinderers lie?**
- **Why was it difficult for the hunters to find the hiders?**
- **What decisions do you need to make soon?**
- **Is God's will difficult to determine?**
- **How do you discover God's will in your life?**
- **What are some of the tactics Satan uses to mislead you?**
- **How can you overcome that?**

You may want to end in prayer or allow small groups to discuss the topic and then pray for each other.

NIGHT LIGHT

Overview: Kids will attempt to locate objects while moving around a darkened room using a small flashlight.

Game Type: Active, discussion-starter, night

Group Size: 2 to 10

Time Involved: 10 to 20 minutes

Supplies: A watch, a penlight or small flashlight, plain paper, paper clips, clear plastic wrap, pieces of thread, loop cereal, a marker, and tape

Preparation: Spread the objects across the room. Tape a long piece of plastic wrap high on one wall. Make sure nothing can be seen when the lights are turned off. On separate sheets of paper, write the following assignments:

- "1. Write your name on a piece of paper."
- "2. Make a paper airplane from the paper you wrote your name on."
- "3. Thread a paper clip and one piece of loop cereal onto a piece of thread."
- "4. Find the clear plastic wrap. Tear off a piece, and bring it to the leader."

Place each assignment sheet in the room near the items kids will need to complete each task.

Gather the group outside the room. Explain that each person will walk a predesigned course in the room, led only by a small flashlight. Point out that there are four tasks kids must accomplish and that they'll find the instructions inside the room.

LEADER TIP

You may want to have players who are waiting talk about times they had to face a problem or situation alone or felt unsure about something.

Say: **You must complete all four tasks and bring finished products with you in the shortest time possible.**

Add that once a player enters the room, he or she may not say anything about the room until the end of the game. This will prevent other players from discovering where activity stations are located.

Start the game, and time each player.

After each person has completed the tasks, declare a winner based on time. Then lead the entire group inside the dark room. Use the flashlight to discuss the following questions:

- How did it feel to enter a dark room with just a small flashlight?
- What happened the longer you stayed in the room?
- Even though your eyes became better adjusted to the dark, did this help in locating the plastic wrap? Why or why not?
- Which do you think was more important: completing all tasks quickly or completing them correctly?

NODDERS

Overview: Kids will use facial expressions to locate objects they see while traveling.

Game Type: No supplies and no preparation, quiet, suitable for disabled, travel

Group Size: Any

Time Involved: 2 to 10 minutes

Supplies: None

Preparation: None

Start the game by assigning facial expressions to *directions*. For example, winking your left eye means "Look to the left side of the vehicle." Have kids practice, making sure everyone is facing the front of the vehicle.

Now add expressions for *objects*, specifically people, places, or things. For example, tilting your head to the left means "person." Again, have kids practice.

You may also wish to incorporate similar expressions or motions for specific traits. For example, tilting your head up means "tall." Players themselves may create other expressions or combinations.

Start with the person seated closest to the driver. He or she should locate something for the other players to name and then use the facial expressions to give directions. See how long it takes someone to guess the object (which probably has passed far from view!). Repeat with other riders until everyone has had a chance to play.

NOT MY ANSWER

Overview: Kids will try to figure out a pattern of answering questions.

Game Type: No supplies and no preparation, quiet, suitable for disabled, travel

Group Size: Any

Time Involved: 10 to 20 minutes

Supplies: None

Preparation: None

This game is designed for teenagers who know each other well. Have the students ask you personal questions, and you will answer as you believe a specific group member might answer. Students will have to guess who you're answering for. The real key in winning the game, however, is to guess the method you're using to choose those you answer for. The method is as follows: You will answer the questions for yourself until someone guesses. Then you'll answer for the person who guesses first. When the students guess correctly who you're answering for, the game starts over again.

Kids might want to ask questions like the following:

- What's your favorite free-time activity?
- Would you rather be rich or famous?
- What is your favorite clothing store?

NUMBER NONSENSE

Overview: Kids will try to guess how you know a number before it's revealed.

Game Type: Quiet, suitable for disabled, travel

Group Size: Any

Time Involved: 2 to 10 minutes

Supplies: Paper and pencils

Preparation: None

Have kids form groups of three or four. Give each group a supply of pencils and paper. Have each group choose a number without revealing the number to you. You will attempt to guess each group's number, and groups will
try to decipher how you suddenly became so smart!

Here's how it works. Suppose the group's number is 16.

Number chosen: 16

Double it: 32

Add 1: 33

Multiply by 5: 165

Add 5: 170

Multiply by 10: 1700

The team announces its number. Then you subtract 100 from the result
without saying anything. For example, 1700 becomes 1600. You then omit the
last two digits and announce that the original number was 16.

OPEN SCISSORS, CLOSED SCISSORS

Overview: Kids will try to figure out how they are to pass the
scissors.

Game Type: Junior high, quiet, suitable for disabled

Group Size: Any

Time Involved: 2 to 10 minutes

Supplies: Scissors

Preparation: None

Have everyone sit in chairs in a circle. Explain to the group that there is a
code to properly passing the scissors and that they have to figure out
whether they are to pass the scissors open or closed. Sit with your legs
crossed, and pass the scissors to the person on your right.

Say: **I received the scissors closed, so I pass the scissors closed.**

That individual must then say, "I receive the scissors closed, so I pass the
scissors [closed or open]." The secret is that if kids are sitting with their legs
crossed in any manner, they must pass the scissors closed; if they're sitting
with their legs open, they must pass the scissors open. If a person passes the
scissors incorrectly, point out that they did so, but continue to the next person anyway. Continue until everyone figures out the secret.

Paper-Plane Relay

Overview: Kids will compete to see who can make the most aeronautically correct paper plane and then will test their skills in a flying relay.

Game Type: Active

Group Size: Any

Time Involved: 10 to 20 minutes

Supplies: Paper

Preparation: None

LEADER TIP

Supply library books on how to make elaborate paper airplanes so kids can research and test new models. You may even want to provide additional supplies to enhance the airplanes, such as tape, paper clips, and markers to decorate the planes.

Have kids form teams of four or five. Give each team several sheets of paper, and tell kids to construct the best paper airplane they can.

Encourage kids to experiment with different airplane designs. Give teams five minutes to complete and test their airplanes and decide on a final design. When kids have finished making their airplanes, have each team present its airplane, explaining why its design is aerodynamically sound.

Then have teams line up on one side of the room. Have the first person in each line hold that team's airplane.

Explain that at your signal, the "pilots" should launch the airplanes into the air, fly the planes to the opposite wall and back, and then pass the planes to the next player in line to repeat the process. If a team's plane is demolished in the process, the team must hurriedly build a new plane and pick up where the first plane was destroyed. The first team to have everyone fly its plane across the room and back wins.

Pig Pen

Overview: Kids will learn to work together to achieve success.

Game Type: Outside, suitable for disabled, team-builder

Group Size: 30 to 50

Time Involved: 20 to 30 minutes

Supplies: Ten 2x4-foot boards per team. (You could use toy water "noodles" instead.)

Preparation: None

Have kids form teams of six, and have each team appoint one person as a "farmer" while the other five will be "pigs." Explain that the farmer has ten gates (represented by the boards or water noodles) and wants to make a pen to separately house each of the five pigs. The pens need to be the same size and shape. Have the teams try to figure out how to build the pens. The first team to do so wins.

Answer:

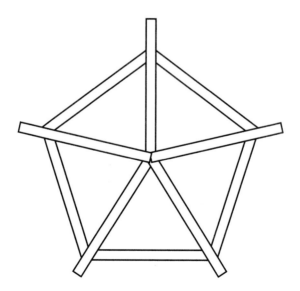

PILLOW SOURCE

Overview: Kids will work together to create a new "invention."

Game Type: Funny, suitable for disabled

Group Size: Any

Time Involved: 20 to 30 minutes

Supplies: A pillowcase and an assortment of odds and ends, such as a rubber band, calculator battery, floppy disk, stapler, sticky note, phone cord, VCR cable, and so on—the crazier and less expensive, the better

Preparation: Place the miscellaneous items in the pillowcase.

Have kids form pairs. Going from pair to pair, allow each teenager to reach into the pillowcase and remove one object. After each person has something in hand, give these instructions:

> Your mission—and you *will* choose to accept it—is for you and your partner to create a new invention using only the objects you have drawn from the pillowcase. No invention is too crazy. Use your imagination, and may the best invention win!

You'll be surprised at what your teenagers come up with. At one recent youth meeting, two teenagers used a rubber band and a playing card to create a "wizzlygog." By winding the rubber band tightly around the card, it would spin wildly when released. Allow each team to demonstrate its invention and, if you like, take a vote for the best of the best.

POSITIVE-ATTRIBUTE BEE

Overview: Kids will focus on how individual positive attributes can be impacted by group processes.

Game Type: Affirmation, discussion-starter, quiet, senior high, suitable for disabled, team-builder

Group Size: 20 to 30

Time Involved: 45 to 60 minutes

Supplies: Paper, scissors, magazines with pictures, colored pens, glue sticks, and large poster board

Preparation: None

Players should select a positive attribute they would like to cultivate within themselves—to become a better listener, a more confident speaker, or more open to change, for example. Then they should create some kind of picture or collage reflecting that attribute.

Next, have each player cut his or her collage into four even diagonal strips. Collect all the strips, mix them all up, and glue them onto poster board to resemble a patchwork quilt. Once you've completed the quilt, have players guess which desired attributes are reflected within it.

Discuss how individual attributes are always present but occasionally obscured within the complexity of the group. Just as we can look at the finished quilt and see evidence of the individual collages, God is able to sift through huge volumes of "crowd noise" and love each of us individually. When we maintain our faith in God's ability to recognize us, we strengthen our ability to recognize one another.

PUZZLER

Overview: Kids will attempt to assemble a paper puzzle while blindfolded.

Game Type: Quiet, suitable for disabled

Group Size: 2 to 10

Time Involved: 2 to 10 minutes

Supplies: A watch, paper, scissors, and a blindfold

Preparation: Cut paper into puzzles of seven to ten pieces each.

Ask for a volunteer, and blindfold him or her. Then display one of the paper puzzles you prepared. Explain that the volunteer is to try to assemble the puzzle as quickly as possible with the help of other group members.

Have others help the volunteer by giving directions on which way a piece should be turned or placed. The volunteer must listen carefully to avoid mistakes. Keep track of time, and repeat with other players and puzzles. The player with the shortest assembly time is the winner.

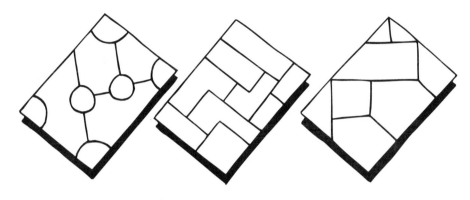

Puzzling Acts

Overview: Kids will quickly look up Bible verses to figure out a Bible puzzle.

Game Type: Bible, knowledge-builder, quiet, suitable for disabled

Group Size: Any

Time Involved: 2 to 10 minutes

Supplies: Bibles, pencils, and the "Puzzling Acts" handout (p. 79)

Preparation: Make photocopies of the "Puzzling Acts" handout (p. 79).

VARIATION

If you wish to energize the game even more, assign one member of each team to go into a different room and look up the first Bible passage there. After finding an answer, he or she will run back to the other team member, who will write down the answer on the handout. Team members can then switch roles.

Have kids form teams of two, and give each team Bibles and a photocopy of the "Puzzling Acts" handout (p. 79).

Say: **Let's see which team can correctly solve the puzzle first. When you're finished with the puzzle, stand up. Ready? Go!**

After everyone has finished the puzzle, ask a volunteer to share the answers.

Here are the answers:

1. Holy Spirit	8. Earthquake
2. Walk	9. Reasoned
3. Stoned	10. Scriptures
4. Blind	11. Eutychus
5. Favoritism	12. Island
6. Angel	13. Boldly
7. Macedonia	Puzzle Answer: Manifestation
	(from 1 Corinthians 12:7)

> ## LEADER TIP
>
> The answers to this puzzle correspond to the New International Version of the Bible. If your kids use a different version, you'll have to rewrite the questions on a chalkboard or on newsprint.

QUICK BACK-DRAW

Overview: Kids will play a draw-on-my-back version of Telephone.

Game Type: Funny, quiet, suitable for disabled

Group Size: 20 to 30

Time Involved: 20 to 30 minutes

Supplies: Paper and pens

Preparation: Draw several objects, each on its own sheet of paper. Be sure the objects are fairly simple—a star, a teddy bear, and an apple, for example.

Puzzling Acts

1. With what did Jesus say the disciples would be baptized (Acts 1:5)?

_____

(two words)

2. What did Peter tell the crippled beggar to do (Acts 3:6)? _____

3. What did the people do to Stephen as he prayed (Acts 7:59)? _____

4. In what condition was Saul after Jesus spoke to him on
the road to Damascus (Acts 9:8-9)? _____

5. While speaking at Cornelius' house, what did Peter realize
that God doesn't show (Acts 10:34-35)? _____

6. Who helped Peter to escape from prison (Acts 12:7)? _____

7. To what country did Paul's vision tell him to go and preach (Acts 16:9-10)?

_____

8. What phenomenon helped Paul and Silas escape from prison (Acts
16:26)?_____

9. What did Paul do in the synagogue to try to persuade people to believe
in Jesus (Acts 18:4)? _____

10. From what did Apollos debate and prove that Jesus was the Christ (Acts
18:28)?_____

11. Who did Paul help revive from death (Acts 20:9-10)? _____

12. According to an angel of God, where would the ship Paul was in run
aground (Acts 27:26)?_____

13. In what manner did Paul teach about Jesus (Acts 28:31)? _____

Puzzle

Now write down the following letters:
- the first letter of the second word from answer 1;
- the first letters from answers 5, 6, 7, 11, and 12;
- the second letters from answers 2, 3, and 13;
- the fourth letters from answers 4, 8, and 10; and
- the sixth letter from answer 9.

Rearrange the letters to form the word that completes this verse from
1 Corinthians 12:7: "Now to each one the _____ of
the Spirit is given for the common good."

Have kids form teams of five. Have these groups sit in straight lines, single file, and face in. Stand in the center of the teams. Thus the lines should look like spokes of a wheel jutting out from the center.

Give the first person in each "spoke" a piece of paper and a pen. Explain that you're going to show the last person in each spoke a picture of an object. They each will then use a finger to draw the object on the back of the person in front of them. Then those people each will draw the object on the back on the person in front of them. This continues up to the first person in each spoke, who then draws on a piece of paper what he or she thinks was drawn. The group that most quickly draws an object most similar to the item you showed them receives a point.

Make sure no one begins drawing until the last person in each spoke has seen the drawing. Then start the game. Let the kids play several times.

Rhyme Time

Overview: Kids will create rhymes until someone is stumped.

Game Type: No supplies and no preparation, quiet, suitable for disabled, travel

Group Size: 10 to 20

Time Involved: 2 to 10 minutes

Supplies: None

Preparation: None

Ask kids to form two teams, and have each team stand in a line facing the opposing team. Tell kids that the object of the game is to keep rhyming for as long as possible.

Say: **The first person on the first team will say a word—car, for example. Then the first person on the opposite team has to say a rhyming word—far, for example. Then the second person on the first team has to say another rhyming word, and play passes back and forth between teams until someone can't rhyme. That person is then out, and his or her team scoots together to make a shorter line. The next player chooses a new word for people to rhyme with. Play continues until one team has no more players.**

To make the game more difficult, ask kids to say a rhyming line of poetry—for example, "I bought a new car. It will go very far. It got caught in some tar" and so on.

RIDDLES AND STUMPERS

Overview: Kids will play a quiz-show-type game to answer riddles and stumpers.

Game Type: Funny, quiet, suitable for disabled

Group Size: 10 to 20

Time Involved: 30 to 45 minutes

Supplies: A watch, paper, pencils, and the "Riddles and Stumpers" handout (p. 82-83)

Preparation: Make photocopies of the "Riddles and Stumpers" handout (p. 82-83), or prepare your own list of riddles and stumpers.

Have the kids form teams of four, and give each team paper and pencils. Have each team designate a team captain who will be responsible for giving the team's answer to each riddle and stumper.

Begin each round by asking each team in rotation the two-part questions on the handout. First ask the riddle, and allow the team ten seconds to confer and give *one* answer. If the team fails to answer correctly within the ten seconds, it receives no points, and play moves to the second team. If the team answers correctly, it earns five points. Then ask the team the stumper question, and allow thirty seconds for the team to confer and answer. If a team answers a stumper correctly, it earns twenty-five points. If the team fails to answer correctly within thirty seconds, it receives no points for the stumper.

When a team misses any question, say the correct answer before moving on to the next team. You may want to lead the kids in a loud "aargh" or "daaah" when reading some of the sillier answers.

Four rounds usually are sufficient to complete the game with fun for all. However, if time allows and if the kids are having fun, continue as long as the supply of riddles and stumpers lasts.

Riddles and Stumpers

Riddle: What is the best paper for making kites?

Answer: Flypaper.

Stumper: An archaeologist reported that he had found an authentic old silver coin inscribed 622 B.C. How do we know he was mistaken?

Answer: How would any coin-maker know that Christ was going to be born in 622 years?

Riddle: Why is the letter "a" like high noon?

Answer: Because it's in the middle of the day.

Stumper: Here are the beginning and the ending of an eleven-letter word. The first three letters and the last three letters are the same. It is an everyday word. What is "und - - - - - und"?

Answer: Underground

Riddle: What has a foot on each end and a foot in the middle?

Answer: A yardstick

Stumper: Is it legal in California for a man to marry his widow's sister?

Answer: It's actually impossible: Only dead men have widows.

Riddle: When is steaming hot soup certain to run out of a good china bowl?

Answer: When there's a *leek* in it.

Stumper: A rowboat can carry only 234 pounds safely. If 235 pounds are put in it, it will be swamped and sink. How can a man weighing 220 pounds and his two sons, one weighing 110 pounds and the other weighing 120 pounds, use the boat to cross the river?

Answer: The two sons go first. One of the sons then brings the boat back and the father rows across alone. Then the other son rows back and gets his brother.

Riddle: Your kitchen sink is overflowing, and soapy water is rapidly flooding the tile floor. Near you are a mop, a bucket, and a screwdriver to open the floor drain. What do you do first to prevent major water damage?

Answer: Turn off the water.

Stumper: A chicken farmer has a special henhouse in which the eggs are collected automatically. Early in the morning, the hens wake up at different times. During this wake-up time, the number of eggs in the collection basket doubles every minute. The first basket will fill with eggs in an hour. When will it be just half full?

Answer: At the end of fifty-nine minutes. The basket must be full at the end of the sixtieth minute, and the number of eggs will double in that last minute.

Riddle: Why is a room full of married people like an empty room?

Answer: Because there's not a *single* person in the room.

Stumper: How is it possible for Nancy to stand behind Larry and Larry to stand behind Nancy at the very same time?

Answer: They stand back to back.

Riddle: Why isn't a human being's nose ever twelve inches long?

Answer: Because then it would be a foot.

Stumper: A wallpaper hanger needs three days to wallpaper a certain room. Then he's asked to wallpaper a room that's twice as long, twice as wide, and twice as high as the first room. Working at his usual rate, how long will it take him to wallpaper the second room?

Answer: Twelve days because he would have to wallpaper four times the space of the first room.

Riddle: What is a difference between a jeweler and a jailer?

Answer: A jeweler sells watches and a jailer watches cells.

Stumper: There are two U.S. coins in a lady's purse. Together they total fifty-five cents. One is not a nickel. What are her two coins?

Answer: A fifty-cent piece and a nickel. (*One* coin is not a nickel, but the other coin is.)

Riddle: Why are fish said to be "brain food"?

Answer: Because they're smart; they live in schools.

Stumper: How can six people divide a sack of six apples equally, without cutting any up, and still have one apple left in the sack?

Answer: They can give the sixth person the sack with the last apple inside.

Riddle: Why is the center of a tree trunk like a dog's tail?

Answer: Because it's farthest from the bark.

Stumper: When tomorrow is yesterday, today will be as near to Sunday as when yesterday was tomorrow. What day is it today?

Answer: Sunday (Tuesday and Friday are each two days away from Sunday.)

RIVER CROSSING

Overview: Kids will work together to figure out how to cross a river.

Game Type: Active, outside, team-builder, water

Group Size: 10 to 20

Time Involved: 10 to 20 minutes

Supplies: Canoes with paddles and life jackets

Preparation: None

Have kids form teams of four. In each team, have one person be the "lion," one be the "donkey," one be the "bail of hay," and one be the "river-crosser." Tell your group that each river-crosser is traveling with three items: a lion, a donkey, and a bail of hay.

Say: **The river-crossers come to a river they have to cross. At the edge of the river is a boat. However, the size of the boat and the speed of the river are such that only one item can be carried across at a time. You need to get all the items across the river intact. The problem is that the lion wants to eat the donkey and the donkey wants to eat the hay. If you're not present, the animals will indulge their desires. Thus, you must ferry them in such a way as to keep them separate on both sides of the river.**

LEADER TIP

While it's fun to play this relay on a river or creek, you can also play on land by setting boundaries as the river.

Begin a relay to see which group can accomplish this first without any animals being eaten!

Here's the solution: First take the donkey across, leaving the lion and the hay. Then take the lion across, leaving the hay. Drop off the lion, but pick up the donkey to take back with you. Drop off the donkey, pick up the hay, and take it across. Then come back one last time for the donkey.

SAME-NAME GAME

Overview: Kids will create different combinations of rhyming words.

Game Type: No supplies and no preparation, quiet, suitable for disabled, travel

Group Size: Any

Time Involved: 10 to 20 minutes

Supplies: None

Preparation: None

Explain to kids that in this game, each person creates a pair of words that rhyme and then develops a two-word clue for the other person to guess. For example, if the clue is "cow wars," the answer would be "cattle battle"; if the answer is "heavy husband," the answer would be "chubby hubby."

Encourage kids to have fun coming up with answers and clues to really stump their partners. You can also have the girls play against the guys or groups play against each other.

Kids can get as simple or elaborate as they want. To throw in a wrinkle, have kids create answers with a biblical tie.

SARDINE SNACKS

Overview: Kids will try to eat standing up in a small room without making a mess.

Game Type: Discussion-starter, food, funny, suitable for disabled, team-builder

Group Size: Any

Time Involved: 2 to 10 minutes

Supplies: Snacks, napkins, and a Bible

Preparation: Find a room that you can uncomfortably but safely cram your group into—a closet, for example.

Have kids stand in the very small space, and show them the snacks.

Say: **You need to try to eat these snacks in this small space, and you can't use your hands or make a mess. There is a way to do this. Your mission is to figure out how.**

Give students no more than ten minutes to complete the game. The way to eat the snacks without making a mess is to cooperate. The kids can't eat their snacks with their own hands, but they can eat their snacks with someone else's hands!

Afterward, let kids out of the small space to discuss their process in solving the problem. Read aloud Mark 9:35, and then tell the following story:

Once there was a great banquet table that seemed to go for miles, and people were sitting on both sides of it. On the table was the most delicious food anyone could ever imagine. But the people sitting at the table were skin and bones; they were starving. They could eat the food only with three-foot-long chopsticks, and they couldn't possibly get the food to their mouths with such long chopsticks. But another group of people were sitting at a different banquet table. The food was just as wonderful. These people also could eat the food only with the three-foot-long chopsticks. But these people were feeding each other across the table with the chopsticks, so everyone was joyful.

This story illustrates the difference between heaven and hell. To be God's servants, we must feed each other first and put ourselves last.

SCRIPTURE PUZZLES

Overview: Kids will learn Bible Scriptures by putting them together as puzzles.

Game Type: Bible, knowledge-builder, quiet, suitable for disabled

Group Size: 20 to 30

Time Involved: 2 to 10 minutes

Supplies: Bibles, tagboard, a marker, scissors, bowls or sacks, and a watch

Preparation: On the tagboard, write Scriptures in large, clear letters. You may want to use Scriptures that pertain to what your group is studying. Then cut each Scripture into puzzle pieces. Place the pieces for each puzzle in a bowl, and place the bowls around the room.

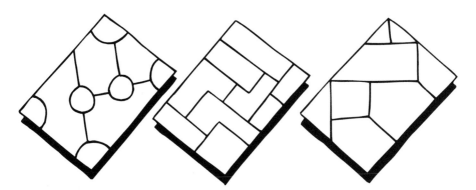

Have kids form teams of four or five, and direct each team to a puzzle. Explain that teams have one minute to put together their puzzles.

Start the game, and then call time after one minute. See which teams have solved their puzzles, and then have teams rotate to different puzzles. Repeat until each team has put together all the puzzles.

VARIATION

Make enough copies of the Scripture passages to have a relay race. Have kids form teams, and provide four puzzles for each team, two at one end of the room and two at the opposite end. Have teams race to solve their puzzles, and declare the team who solves four puzzles first the winner.

SHAKERS!

Overview: Kids will shake a capped pill bottle to guess what types of objects are inside.

Game Type: Quiet, suitable for disabled, travel

Group Size: Any

Time Involved: 2 to 10 minutes

Supplies: Several large plastic pill or vitamin bottles (non-transparent) with caps and small amounts of dry beans, rice, rocks, marbles, coins, paper clips, or cotton balls

Preparation: Fill each bottle half full with one of the items, such as paper clips in one, beans in another, and so on. Place the cap securely on the bottle.

Gather kids in a circle, and display the filled bottles. Explain that each person will have a chance to shake a bottle once and try to figure out what it contains. Add that no one may guess until everyone has shaken the bottle.

Once the bottle has been passed around the circle, call for guesses. There may be several different answers. Narrow responses until reaching one accepted by the entire group. Then open the bottle and reveal the contents.

Declare the group successful if it guessed the correct answer, or give another chance by using a different bottle. Repeat until kids have guessed the contents of all the bottles.

Sing a New Song

Overview: Kids will create new lyrics to familiar hymns.

Game Type: Musical, suitable for disabled

Group Size: 2 to 10

Time Involved: 20 to 30 minutes

Supplies: Hymnals and a piano or keyboard, if you have musicians in your group

Preparation: None

Have kids form small groups, and give each group hymnals. Tell groups to use their creativity to come up with new lyrics for hymns. Also encourage kids to create a new style for the hymns—one that still works with the new lyrics. For example, a group could alter the lyrics to "Amazing Grace" and then sing it as a rap.

After kids have had a few minutes to create their songs, have them perform for everyone.

SLAPPIN' SILLY

Overview: Kids will slap balloons into goals.

Game Type: Active

Group Size: 10 to 20

Time Involved: 2 to 10 minutes

Supplies: Balloons, two large trash cans, and a watch

Preparation: Inflate the balloons.

This game is best played in a large room with no noticeable wind currents. Position the two trash cans at opposite ends of the room to serve as goals. Make sure the trash cans are large enough to hold two totally inflated balloons.

You'll play this game in three rounds. The first round will familiarize your kids with the game. The second two rounds—described later—will engage your kids' strategic thinking.

Round 1

Position your kids in a grid pattern with at least three feet between them. Have kids sit cross-legged on the floor. The diagram assumes you have twelve kids in your youth group. Adjust the pattern if you have more or less than that number.

The objective is to move balloons from your back court to your opponents' goal and to get the balloons into the other team's basket. Players must obey the following rules:

- You can't leave your position (no scooting!).
- You can grab a balloon and hold it, but you can move it only by slapping it.
- You can't deflate balloons.

Use at least twenty balloons for nine kids. The more balloons, the more confusion, and the harder it is to play both offense and defense simultaneously. The game ends when either team has two different colored balloons in the opposing team's wastebasket.

Round 2

Allow one team to add *one rule* to the game to increase the likelihood they'll win. However, *both* teams must enforce the rule. For instance, the rule might be that all blue-eyed players must sit on their hands, but blue-eyed players on *both* teams must obey the rule. Whether that rule would be a strategic advantage or disadvantage would depend on how many blue-eyed people are on each team.

Allow teams to huddle separately for up to ninety seconds to determine what rule they wish to create, and then ask players to resume playing positions. Ask for the additional rule to be clearly stated for round 2, and then have kids play the game.

Round 3

Allow the other team to add a new rule. Again, allow teams to huddle separately for up to ninety seconds to determine what rule they wish to create, and then ask players to resume playing positions. Ask for the new rule to be clearly stated, and then play round 3 with that rule in force.

SNIFF-FEST

Overview: Kids will work together to guess what flavors of dog and cat foods they are sniffing.

Game Type: Funny, suitable for disabled

Group Size: Any

Time Involved: 10 to 20 minutes

Supplies: Various dog and cat foods

Preparation: Arrange samples of various dog and cat foods on a table in a room different from where you'll be meeting. Label or code the dog and cat foods if you'll have trouble remembering their flavors. Flavors might include liver, fish, beef, chicken, or other exotic delicacies.

Have kids form teams of two or three. Then invite one team at a time to enter the room while blindfolded and sniff the various samples of dog or cat food. You may also wish to have an adult guide help the youth make their way. Allow the kids to touch the food or—for the very brave—taste it!

As each team exits the room, give the team a piece of paper and a pencil, and ask them to come to a consensus as to the flavor of dog or cat food they sniffed.

> **LEADER TIP**
>
> If you like, give a dog bone or chew toy as a trophy to the team that has the most correct answers.

SNOWING

Overview: Kids will work to strategically eliminate letters while creating words.

Game Type: Quiet, suitable for disabled

Group Size: 20 to 30

Time Involved: 2 to 10 minutes

Supplies: A room with several windows in it, canned snow, paper, pencils, and a damp cloth

Preparation: On each window, write the word "snowing" with the canned snow.

Have your kids form the same number of groups as you have windows.

Say: **Once upon a time, a bored youth director woke up and saw that it was snowing outside. He wrote the word "snowing" on his window; then for fun he rubbed out one of the letters. He realized he had created a new word. He rubbed out another letter and still had a real word. He continued this way until he had only one letter left, and that was still a word. As a team, work out the order in which he erased the letters and what words he created. Have one person on your team be the recorder and write down your answers.**

Solution:

N Sowing
O Swing
W Sing
G Sin
S In
N I

SPEECH! SPEECH!

Overview: Kids will have only twenty words and thirty seconds to make a speech.

Game Type: Funny, quiet, suitable for disabled, travel

Group Size: 2 to 10

Time Involved: 2 to 10 minutes

Supplies: A watch

Preparation: None

Appoint an official word-counter and an official timer, or assume one of the roles yourself. Then explain that each player will have exactly twenty words and thirty seconds to present a speech on a topic you give him or her. Give each new player a different topic.

To win, the player must make a logical speech about the subject, ending with the words "the end." If the player uses more or fewer than twenty words or takes more than thirty seconds, he or she is out of the running. It's OK to take less than thirty seconds.

Any players left in the game after everyone has had a turn will play a tie-breaking round using new subjects. After the second round of speeches, the rest of the kids will vote for the best speech. If no one makes it to the second round, give everyone another turn. With a little practice, kids can really improve their speaking abilities!

Use topics that will be familiar to your students. Some possible broad topics include the following:

- recent group or church activities
- movies
- TV shows
- food categories

- animals
- sports
- school subjects

STEPPINGSTONES

Overview: Kids will try to "walk" on water.

Game Type: Active, outside, water

Group Size: 2 to 10

Time Involved: 10 to 20 minutes

Supplies: Water, a child's swimming pool for each team, three coffee cans with lids for each team, sand, and three four-foot boards for each team.

Preparation: Fill the coffee cans with sand, and place lids on them. Fill the children's pools with water, and place three cans just outside the edge of each of the pools.

Have kids form teams of four to six to figure out how to configure the coffee cans and planks of wood so that team members can cross the water. However, no plank of wood may reach between two coffee cans.

Say: **Your job as a team is to figure out a way to arrange the three planks so that someone can cross from one "steppingstone" to either of the other two without getting wet.**

Let the teams start trying to figure out the solution; the first team that does so wins. Although there may be different solutions, here's one.

Straw Towers

Overview: Kids will try to make the tallest self-supporting structure out of drinking straws.

Game Type: Quiet, suitable for disabled

Group Size: Any

Time Involved: 2 to 10 minutes

Supplies: A watch, tape, and drinking straws

Preparation: None

Have kids form teams of six, and give each team fifty to one hundred drinking straws and two rolls of tape. Explain that teams must create as tall a free-standing structure as they can in ten minutes.

Start the game, and call time after ten minutes. Then have each group present its structure, and determine which is the highest.

Swamp Crossing

Overview: Kids will try to be the first to cross a "swamp" by going over "rocks."

Game Type: Active, suitable for disabled, team-builder

Group Size: Any

Time Involved: 30 to 45 minutes

Supplies: Construction paper, scissors, and string

Preparation: Use the string to mark a starting line and a finish line about fifteen to twenty feet apart. Cut out three 1½-square-foot pieces of construction paper for each team.

Have kids form two to four teams, and give each team three "rocks" (construction paper).

Explain that between the starting line and finish line is nothing but water that is too thick to swim in and too deep to stand up in. Instruct the teams that they're in a race to get across the water first. They're allowed to use the three "rocks" to get everyone across the water safely. The catch is that each person can have only one foot on a rock at a time. If someone puts two feet on a rock or steps into the water, the whole team has to start over. Kids can move the rocks as they go along, and two or more people can have one foot each on a single rock, but at no time can a single person have both feet on a single rock. The first team to successfully get their entire group across the water wins.

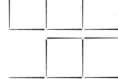

TOOTHPICK TANGLE

Overview: Kids will compete to see who can untangle toothpick puzzles.

Game Type: Quiet, suitable for disabled

Group Size: Any

Time Involved: 10 to 20 minutes

Supplies: Toothpicks (The colorful plastic ones work best.)

Preparation: None

Kids can play this game in pairs or individually.

Give each player (or pair) a supply of at least twelve toothpicks. Then see who can solve the following toothpick problems first.

1. Toothpick Triangles

The problem: Have players make four triangles out of six tooth-picks.

The solution: One triangle is made flat on the table, point facing down. Then place two toothpicks on top like a roof and the other toothpick down the center vertically.

2. Subtracting Squares

The problem: Make three squares using ten toothpicks. Then subtract two toothpicks and leave two squares.

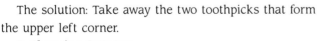

The solution: Take away the two toothpicks that form the upper left corner.

3. Changing Squares

The problem: Show kids how to arrange twelve toothpicks in four squares as shown on page 96. Then have kids rearrange the toothpicks, using them all but moving only three of them to change the four squares to three.

The solution: Remove the two toothpicks that form the upper left corner, as before, plus the lower right horizontal toothpick. Use them to form a new square at the lower right, as shown.

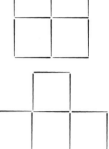

Toy Guy Solutions

Overview: Kids will use toy people to play out world problems.

Game Type: Discussion-starter, suitable for disabled

Group Size: 10 to 20

Time Involved: 30 to 45 minutes

Supplies: Plastic army people (available in toy stores), paper, and markers

Preparation: At the top of each sheet of paper, write a world problem, such as war, poverty, greed, irresponsibility, and oppression.

As teenagers enter the room, ask them to sign in under one of the world problems. Then have all the kids that signed the same posters form groups. Give each group a set of army figures.

Say: **This toy teaches that the way to solve problems is to fight. But we've tried that for a long time, and the problems are still here. What would God say? What is the solution to your problem? Use your army guys to demonstrate a true-to-life solution and how it would work. For example, you can move the guys and explain your strategy or set up a scene with your army guys. Just dream big and dream specifically.**

Give groups a while to discuss the problems. While groups work, ask questions such as the following:

- How has this problem historically played itself out?
- What are the problem's root causes?
- What might change it?
- What role might God want you to play personally in this solution—through your occupation, leadership, or a campaign, for example.

Have each team present its solution. Highlight any innovative and truly biblical ideas. Agree that the solutions are seldom easy, but that each person can make a difference.

Triple Square

Overview: Groups will arrange themselves to form three identical squares that are touching each other.

Game Type: Active, no supplies and no preparation

Group Size: 30 to 50

Time Involved: 20 to 30

Supplies: None

Preparation: None

In this game, based on a matchstick puzzle, players become the "matchsticks." Have kids form teams of twelve to eighteen, and then have twelve members in each team play the matchsticks. Have the matchsticks lie down to form the number symbol. (See illustration on p. 98.) Explain that everyone—both the matchsticks and the other team members—should try to figure out which *three* matchsticks need to move to make three identical squares that are touching each other.

Allow one matchstick at a time to come out of the formation, take a look from a distance, and see if he or she can figure out who needs to move. The team that solves the puzzle first wins. However, even after one team has solved the puzzle, have the other teams keep trying.

> ### LEADER TIP
> You might want to provide team members who aren't matchsticks with real matchsticks to manipulate. If a team is having trouble, you can also tell it that only the corners of the three squares will touch.

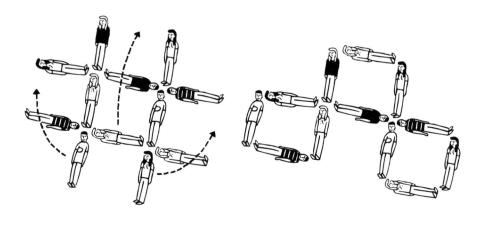

TUNE TIME

Overview: Kids will review a little science as they guess tunes played on water glasses.

Game Type: Musical, suitable for disabled

Group Size: Any

Time Involved: 20 to 30 minutes

Supplies: A pitcher of water and eight drinking glasses per team, and pencils

Preparation: None

Have kids form teams of one to eight players. Give each team a partially filled pitcher of water and eight drinking glasses. Also provide a pencil for each player.

Demonstrate your musical talent by pouring a little water into one of the glasses and then gently but firmly striking the side of the glass with the pencil. You'll hear a musical tone. Then pour the water back into the pitcher.

Tell teams to pour water into their glasses and tune the eight glasses to the eight notes of the diatonic or "do-re-mi" scale. Kids will need to experiment with different amounts of water in the glasses to get the notes right.

When teams have tuned the glasses to their

> **LEADER TIP**
>
> You may want to explain to kids that the more water is in the glass, the deeper the tone will be.

satisfaction, have each team think of a song to try to stump the other teams. Tell kids to make sure all teammates have a part in playing the song. Let kids practice for a while, and then have them play their songs for each other. The first team to correctly name each song gets a point.

After all teams have performed, have teams choose new songs and play again.

TWISTED CIRCLE

Overview: Kids will try to untangle a twisted circle.

Game Type: Active, no supplies and no preparation

Group Size: 20 to 30

Time Involved: 20 to 30 minutes

Supplies: None

Preparation: None

Have kids form groups of six, and have each group choose one person to be the "puzzler." Ask the puzzlers to leave the room.

Explain that each group should form a circle and hold hands. Then each group should form a human knot by walking over and under and around each other—but should always keep holding hands.

After groups have had a few minutes to twist up, call the puzzlers back in. Ask the puzzlers to untangle the knots their group members have created. Tell the puzzlers that group members must never let go of each other's hands.

After the puzzlers have completed their task, have kids switch roles and play again.

TWISTER WORKOUT

Overview: Kids will try to repeat tongue twisters in rapid succession without stumbling.

Game Type: Funny, no supplies and no preparation, suitable for disabled, travel

Group Size: Any

Time Involved: 10 to 20 minutes

Supplies: None

Preparation: None

This game is sure to bring laughter to your group. Have your group get into circles of five to seven people.

Say: **I will give each of your groups a tongue twister, and, one at a time, you will repeat the tongue twister as fast as you can five times. If you stumble over any word, you must drop out of that round. The object of the game is to see how many of these tongue twisters you can successfully pronounce.**

Tongue Twisters:
Shall she sell seashells by the seashore?
Adam added aardvarks.
Was Thaddaeus the third disciple?
Armageddon armies of Antichrist
Babylon babies babbled.
Timothy's Thessalonian thanksgiving
Esau saw stew.
Shepherds sheer sheep.
Cherubim cherish the child.

VERY PUNNY

Overview: Kids will use their creativity to create puns.

Game Type: Discussion-starter, funny, quiet, suitable for disabled

Group Size: Any

Time Involved: 10 to 20 minutes

Supplies: Paper and pencils

Preparation: None

Have kids form groups of five; distribute paper and pencils.

Then say: **The object of this game is to create the cleverest alternative definitions, or puns, for some words you might have heard in church. You'll have ten minutes to come up with definitions for the** words I give you. Then you'll share your definitions with everyone.

One by one, read aloud the following terms so kids can copy them onto paper:

- salvation
- Lamentations
- redemption
- Pentecost
- synagogue
- theology
- atonement
- altar
- tabernacle
- evangelism

After all the groups have presented their puns, ask the following questions:

- **Why was this game difficult?**
- **How do you think visitors might feel when we use words like this at church?**
- **What could we do to make visitors feel more welcome at our church?**

WATCH OUT

Overview: Kids will test their powers of observation with watches.

Game Type: Quiet, suitable for disabled, travel

Group Size: Any

Time Involved: 10 to 20 minutes

Supplies: Watches

Preparation: None

Have kids form teams of five, and make sure each team has at least one player with a watch.

Say: **Now trade watches with other teams. I want each of you to spend two minutes studying the watch in your group and pay attention to as many details as you can.**

After each team has studied its watch, say:

Now turn in your watches to me, and answer the following questions. I'll give each team thirty seconds to answer the questions correctly. The group with the most correct answers will be our winner.
- What brand is your watch?
- What color is the wristband?
- What time was it when you handed the watch to me?
- Does the watch display the date?
- Does the watch display the day?
- Who is the owner of your group's watch?
- Where was the watch manufactured?
- Is it a quartz watch?
- Does the watch display seconds?
- Does the watch have an alarm?

WATER-BALLOON OLYMPICS

Overview: Kids will test their skill and strength in this collection of games using water balloons.

Game Type: Active, messy, outside, water

Group Size: Any

Time Involved: 10 to 20 minutes

Supplies: Water balloons, water, buckets

Preparation: Fill balloons with water, and tie them off.

Use the following ideas for some hot-weather fun with your kids.

What's your angle? See how accurately teams can gauge angles and velocity in this water balloon-tossing test. Place a plastic bucket against a wall for each team, and have teams line up single file five or more feet from the buckets. Let kids take turns tossing their water balloons against the wall above the buckets. The goal is to have the water balloons break above the buckets and for the water to fall into the buckets. The team with the most water in its bucket when you call time wins.

Hold that thought. Have kids kneel in a circle, facing in. If you have a large group, have kids form several circles. Each circle should have no more than eight kids.

Place a water balloon on the ground in front of each player. Kids will do push-ups over their water balloons. The catch is that each person in the circle will do only one push-up at a time, with players holding themselves in push-up position over the water balloons until their turns come again. Obviously, the winner in each circle will be the player who hasn't dropped onto a water balloon. Losers in this game should be easy to spot!

WATER SCRAMBLE

Overview: Kids will compete to place a full glass of water the farthest distance they can.

Game Type: Team-builder

Group Size: Any

Time Involved: 20 to 30 minutes

Supplies: Masking tape, water, and glasses

Preparation: Fill the glasses completely full with water, and put some masking tape across the floor to represent a "penalty line."

Have kids form teams of five. Give each team a glass of water that is filled to the rim. Explain that team members will work together to see who can place their glass of water farthest into the "penalty area." Add that team members may not touch the penalty area with any part of their body.

Say: **You'll need to work together to place or slide the glass of water as far on the other side of the line as you can without touching the ground and without spilling water. The winning team will not only be the one that gets their glass the farthest into the penalty area, but will also be the one that has the most water left in the glass.**

Allow the teams about five minutes to develop strategies; then choose one group to go first. Mark each team's spot with a piece of masking tape.

There isn't a specific strategy that seems to be the "best" way of doing this. Rather, this game allows students to use their creativity and skills.

What Is the Word?

Overview: Kids will reverse the normal use of the dictionary and test their vocabulary.

Game Type: Quiet, suitable for disabled

Group Size: 10 to 20

Time Involved: 20 to 30 minutes

Supplies: A dictionary, a watch, paper, and a pen

Preparation: None

Have kids form teams of about four, with a maximum number of four teams. Explain that each team will be allowed ten seconds to identify the word that matches exactly the definition you read. Team members may confer before answering, but only the first answer given will be accepted. They'll score one point for each correct answer. Add that the dictionary used in the game will be the final authority in the event of any disputes or questions.

Read aloud a definition, and ask the team to name the word. Do not give more than one team the same question, even if a team has failed to answer correctly. Keep the game moving along quickly.

If teams tie, continue the game until one team guesses a word incorrectly in a round in which the other team guesses correctly.

What's It Worth?

Overview: Kids will test their shopping savvy in this game of price wars.

Game Type: Quiet, suitable for disabled

Group Size: 10 to 20

Time Involved: 10 to 20 minutes

Supplies: Advertising circulars, scissors, paper, and a pencil

Preparation: Make photocopies of the advertising circulars found in the Sunday newspaper. Then cut out pictures of items for sale (without the prices showing), and keep the copies for yourself as price references.

Have kids form two teams. Have the first players from each team sit at a table facing each other. Show the players the picture of an item for sale. Have players name a dollar amount they think is closest to the actual price of the item.

Players alternate guessing how much the item costs. Each player gets up to three guesses. Encourage players' teammates to call out advice as to whether to guess a higher or lower price. If a player thinks he or she is close to the actual price and doesn't want to guess anymore, that player should shout, "What's it worth?" to stop the bidding.

At that point, the last guess made by each player stands. Reveal the actual price by showing the copy of the advertisement for that item. The team that guessed closest to the actual price gets a point. Keep score as each player gets a chance to guess on a new item. The team with the highest score after everyone has had a turn wins.

WHAT'S THE AMOUNT?

Overview: Kids will try to be the first team to add up a series of numbers.

Game Type: Active, knowledge-builder, suitable for disabled

Group Size: 10 to 20

Time Involved: 10 to 20 minutes

Supplies: Index cards and pens

Preparation: Write out a series of math equations on separate index cards. For example, write "1 +" on a card, "2 -" on a card, "3 +" on a card, and so on. Make up to twenty cards with varying equations of low to higher difficulty. Make two sets of cards, and be sure you know the final answer to each set.

Have kids form teams of two or three, and place each team behind a designated starting point. At the other end of the room, place a chair in front of each team, and place equation cards on each chair. Also place some blank index cards and a pen at each chair so kids can write their answers.

Say: **When I say "go," the first person will race to the chair, read an equation card, and write the sum on a blank index card. Then that person will race back to the team and tag the next person. The second** person will race to the chair, read the next equation card, and write the new total on the index card. The team who arrives at the correct answer first wins.

WHAT'S UP WITH THAT?

Overview: Kids will decipher the meaning of word puzzles.

Game Type: Quiet, suitable for disabled

Group Size: Any

Time Involved: 10 to 20 minutes

Supplies: "Word Pictures" handout (p. 107) and pencils

Preparation: Make photocopies of the "Word Pictures" handout (p. 107).

Give each student in your group a copy of the "Word Pictures" handout (p. 107) and a pencil. Give the group ten minutes to come up with as many of the phrases hidden on the handout as possible.

Answers:
1. The Ten Commandments
2. Pillar of salt
3. Sea of Galilee
4. Forty days and forty nights
5. The last shall be first
6. Empty Tomb
7. In the beginning was the Word
8. Mount Sinai (Sign eye)
9. First, second, and third John
10. Jars of clay
11. Jacob's ladder
12. Amazing grace
13. Coat of Many Colors
14. The last days
15. In the beginning, God...

Word Pictures

X Rules	N a C l	^aG l i i l e e e	XXXX a.m. XXXX p.m.
Last	MT 2M	B°E°G°I°N N I N G	MT
John John John		J a c o b ' s	G R A C E

BLUE RED GREEN YELLOW ORANGE BLACK	Days, Days, **Days**	God

WHICH CAME FIRST?

Overview: Kids will assemble puzzle pieces in the form of either a bird or an egg.

Game Type: Quiet, suitable for disabled

Group Size: Any

Time Involved: 2 to 10 minutes

Supplies: The egg pattern below, scissors, and envelopes

Preparation: Make photocopies of the pattern, cut the pieces apart, and place each pattern in an envelope.

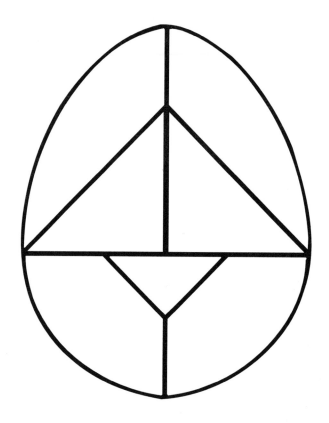

Have kids form groups of between two and six players.

Say: **Inside each envelope are the exact same pieces. These pieces can be used to form a lot of different creature forms. But today your task is to answer the age-old question "Which came first: the chicken or the egg?" Work together as a group to form either a bird or an egg using all the pieces, and we'll see which really comes first.**

Allow the players to explore with the pieces, and accept any solution that comes close to looking like a bird or egg, as long as all the pieces are used.

WILL THE REAL BIBLE CHARACTER PLEASE STAND UP?

Overview: Kids will stretch their knowledge of Bible characters by playing a guessing game.

Game Type: Bible, discussion-starter, knowledge-builder, mixer, suitable for disabled

Group Size: Any

Time Involved: 20 to 30 minutes

Supplies: Bibles, paper, and a pen

Preparation: Create a list of questions about several biblical characters, and create three different scripts for each character, one script that is accurate and two scripts that are slightly inaccurate. See the example below.

Before the activity, enlist three people to present each set of scripts. Explain to them that only one of them will play the true biblical character and that the other two must play a convincing impostor.

LEADER TIP

As an interesting twist, have the biblical characters wear costumes. Or have some characters wear costumes and some wear modern clothing to further confuse the guessers.

Have the three characters sit in front of the group. Pass out the questions you prepared to volunteers from the group, and inform kids that only one of the three biblical characters is real. The group must discover which is the real Bible character by asking each character the questions and listening carefully to the responses.

For example, if the group is trying to find Paul, here is a sample question with three sample scripts (with the errors italicized):

Question: Tell us about your conversion experience.

Script 1 (impostor): "As I was walking on the road to Damascus, a voice cried out to me, '*Paul, Paul,* why are you persecuting me?' It was Jesus, and I decided to follow him."

Script 2 (impostor): "As I was walking on the road to *Tarsus,* a voice cried out to me, 'Saul, Saul, why are you persecuting me?' It was Jesus, and I decided to follow him."

Script 3 (Paul): "As I was walking on the road to Damascus, a voice cried out to me, 'Saul, Saul, why are you persecuting me?' It was Jesus, and I decided to follow him."

These are simple examples. You can make the scripts elaborate and detailed, or you can keep them simple.

Use this game to lead into a discussion about the subtlety of false prophets.

WORD BIRTHDAYS

Overview: Kids will discover the birthdays of several words unique to the twentieth century.

Game Type: Quiet, suitable for disabled

Group Size: Any

Time Involved: 2 to 10 minutes

Supplies: The "Word Birthdays" handout (p. 111) and pencils

Preparation: Make photocopies of the "Word Birthdays" handout (p. 111).

This team game will test your group's knowledge of twentieth-century words. Give each player a copy of the "Word Birthdays" handout (p. 111), and see who can correctly match the most dates with words.

Answers:

1905—vitamin	1947—apartheid
1928—penicillin	1951—discotheque
1930—teenager	1958—aerospace
1931—microwave	1961—mini
1942—astronavigation	1971—bioethics
1944—aerosol	1979—siliconitis

Word Birthdays

1905	aerosol
1928	mini
1930	bioethics
1931	penicillin
1942	teenager
1944	astronavigation
1947	discotheque
1951	vitamin
1958	aerospace
1961	siliconitis
1971	microwave
1979	apartheid

Friend-Making Games

ALL PARTS OF ONE BODY

Overview: Kids will try to accomplish a task by working together as "body parts."

Game Type: Active, Bible, discussion-starter, senior high, suitable for disabled, team-builder

Group Size: Any

Time Involved: 20 to 30 minutes

Supplies: Bibles, water, and plastic foam cups

Preparation: Fill the cups with water, and set the cups and the Bibles on a table.

Have kids form teams of no fewer than five and no more than ten. Assign each member of each team a body part—eyes, ears, mouths, brains, legs, arms, and hands, for example. Assign body parts depending on the size of each group as well as the activity they will perform, but make sure you assign the brain, eyes, mouth, legs, and arms.

Explain that you'll give teams a task to do, and then they'll race to see which team can complete it the fastest. Explain that on each team, kids can perform only the function of their body part.

Assign each group to walk across the room to drink a cup of water. This means the legs have to carry over the mouth and the hands, then the hand has to pick up the water, and the mouth has to drink it. Thus all team members have to work together to accomplish the task.

After teams have accomplished the first task, have them try a more advanced exercise. Have them walk to a Bible, pick it up, and read a verse out loud.

Afterward, discuss how each member of a church or youth group is important and must work together as part of Christ's body. Read aloud Romans 12:4-6a, and ask:

- What was frustrating about this game?
- How does the Scripture reflect the game?
- Why is it so important to work together?
- How can we work together as members of the body of Christ?

AND THE NAME IS?

Overview: Kids will try to call out each other's names the fastest.

Game Type: Funny, no supplies and no preparation, suitable for disabled

Group Size: 20 to 30

Time Involved: 2 to 10 minutes

Supplies: None

Preparation: None

Have kids sit in a circle and each say their first and last names. Then have kids form two teams.

Say: **In this game, you'll earn points for your team if you can be the first person to call out another person's name. Each team will stand on one side of the door. One person from the team will stand in the doorway before the door is opened. When the door is opened, the first person to shout out the other person's name gets ten points for his or her team. Then we'll shut the door and play again. You can switch people around as much as you want.**

Start the game, and have teams keep track of their points. Play several times to help kids learn each other's names.

> ## VARIATION
>
> You can switch up the game by asking kids to recall first, middle, and last names; eye colors; or grade levels.

ANIMAL SQUAWKS

Overview: Kids will form pairs based on animal sounds and behaviors.

Game Type: Funny, icebreaker, mixer, suitable for disabled

Group Size: Any

Time Involved: 2 to 10 minutes

Supplies: Two bowls, index cards, and markers

Preparation: Write the name of an animal on two index cards. Then on one of the cards, write the sound the animal makes; on the other card, write one of the animal's behaviors. For example, you could write, "Dog, bark" on one card and "Dog, wag tail" on another card. Repeat the process with different animals, and make enough cards so each person in the group will have one. Place all the animal sound cards in one bowl and all the animal behavior cards in another bowl.

Have kids form two groups. Ask one group to select cards from the "animal sounds" bowl and the other group to select cards from the "animal behaviors" bowl. Tell kids to read their cards to themselves.

Explain that when you say "go," everyone must begin making the animal sound or acting out the animal behavior from their card. Then each person should go around the room and look for his or her animal "match."

Start the game, and be prepared for a lot of noise and commotion! When matches have found each other, have pairs sit down and think of their animals' positive characteristics—otters are industrious, dogs are loyal, cats are independent, for example. Each pair can then stand and tell the group about their animal—and provide a demonstration of its sound and behavior!

AUTOBIOGRAPHICAL CATCH

Overview: Kids will toss around a ball and tell about themselves in a fast-paced manner.

Game Type: Funny, suitable for disabled

Group Size: Any

Time Involved: 10 to 20 minutes

Supplies: A watch and at least one ball

Preparation: None

Have your group sit in a circle. If you have more than twelve students in your group, have kids form several circles.

Say: **I have several questions that will help us get to know each other better. Here's how we'll play. I'll toss a ball to someone in the** circle, and that person will have to answer a question I ask in less than thirty seconds. Then he or she should toss the ball to someone who hasn't answered a question yet.

Questions:

- What is your greatest accomplishment in life?
- What was your happiest day ever? Tell us about it.
- What is your most treasured possession, and why?
- If you could create a phrase to print on a T-shirt, what would it be?
- Who is your hero?
- What is your favorite sport?
- What animal best reflects your personality?
- Who is your favorite relative, and why?
- What is the best thing that ever happened to you at church?
- What is your biggest dream?
- What would you want your tombstone to say about you?
- How would your friends describe you?

BAGGIES

Overview: Kids will work in teams to stuff garbage bags full of trash.

Game Type: Active, junior high, outside, service, suitable for disabled

Group Size: Any

Time Involved: 2 to 10 minutes

Supplies: Large plastic trash bags and a watch

Preparation: Scout out an area close to your meeting area that could use some cleanup.

Have kids form teams of three, and give each team a trash bag. Explain that on your signal, teams will begin racing to fill their bags with trash they find. Give kids a time limit (a shorter time limit is better for junior high kids), and then start the game. When time is up, declare the team that collected the most trash the winner.

BANANARAMA

Overview: Kids will attempt to feed each other bananas while tied together.

Game Type: Food, funny, suitable for disabled

Group Size: Any

Time Involved: 2 to 10 minutes

Supplies: Bananas, scissors, and string or ribbon

Preparation: None

Have kids form pairs, and tie each pair's left wrists together with string. Give each person a banana, and tell kids they must peel their bananas and feed them to their partners. The first pair to successfully eat both of its bananas wins.

BASEBALL BONANZA

Overview: Kids will play a variation of America's favorite pastime in which they can't stop.

Game Type: Active, outside

Group Size: 20 to 30

Time Involved: 20 to 30 minutes

Supplies: Four bases and a rubber ball

Preparation: Create a diamond-shaped infield as in softball. Place the four bases about thirty feet apart.

Have kids form two teams. Explain that the batters will take turns standing at home base, tossing the ball into the air, and hitting the ball with an open hand. Then each batter will run around the bases in the usual order, but they must make the complete circuit back to home without stopping.

Tell kids that the only way a batter is out is if an opposing team member catches the batter's fly ball or throws the ball to any base ahead of the batter.

Add that the outfield team must throw the ball to first base, then second, then third, and then home in an attempt to get the ball to a base ahead of the batter. The baseman must have his or her foot on the base before throwing the ball to the next base.

Every team member should have a turn at bat. You may use a nine-inning, three-out basis, or make up your own rules. The team that scores the most runs wins.

BIBLE PING-PONG

Overview: Kids will learn each other's full names as they volley a Ping-Pong ball.

Game Type: Active, suitable for disabled

Group Size: Any

Time Involved: 2 to 10 minutes

Supplies: Bibles and Ping-Pong balls

Preparation: None

Give each player a Bible, and have kids form groups of five to ten. Then ask each group's members to stand in a circle facing each other.

Say: **The object of this game is to work together as a team to spell correctly the full names of each person in the group. Each person should grip the Bible, palms up, with both hands. One person will begin the game by using the Bible to hit a Ping-Pong ball to someone else in the circle. The first person to receive a volley needs to say the first letter of his or her own name while hitting the ball to someone else. The game continues as each person receiving a volley adds the next letter of the first person's name while hitting the ball to someone else. If your group fails to completely spell the person's name, you should start over until you have successfully volleyed a person's entire name—first, middle, and last. The group may then start over spelling someone else's name as they volley the Ping-Pong ball. No player may hit the ball two times in a row.**

After you have explained the game, allow kids to familiarize themselves with each other's full names, including the spellings. Then give one player in each group a Ping-Pong ball to begin playing.

Bingo Brouhaha

Overview: Kids will learn what others like and dislike while playing this fun variation of Bingo.

Game Type: Mixer, suitable for disabled

Group Size: Any

Time Involved: 10 to 20 minutes

Supplies: Pencils and the "Bingo Brouhaha" handout (p. 121)

Preparation: Make photocopies of the "Bingo Brouhaha" handout (p. 121).

Distribute the pencils and "Bingo Brouhaha" handouts (p. 121).

Say: **The object of this game is to be the first person to get a "bingo" with five different names. Walk around the room and collect signatures of people who agree with a statement on your bingo card. You may get only one signature from each player, and you may not use your own name. When you've filled five consecutive spaces, shout out "Bingo!"**

BINGO
Brouhaha

Loves soccer	Owns a car	Plays piano	Has blue eyes	Likes beans
Has a dog	Hates cats	Loves art	Plays video games	Has a personal computer
Has a girlfriend or boyfriend	Loves God	**FREE SPACE**	Hates homework	Plays guitar
Has a stereo	Has 20/20 vision	Loves school	Hates rice	Has blond hair
Keeps bedroom clean	Has small feet	Surfs the Net	Sings in the car	Sleeps with a stuffed animal

BITTY BITTY BUM

Overview: Player will attempt to introduce the person next to him or her before someone can say, "Bitty bitty bum."

Game Type: Junior high, no supplies and no preparation, suitable for disabled

Group Size: Any

Time Involved: 2 to 10 minutes

Supplies: None

Preparation: None

Have everyone sit in a circle, and ask one volunteer to sit in the middle of the circle. Give everyone about one minute to get to know the names of the individuals on both sides of them. Then start the game.

The person in the middle is to point to anyone in the circle and say either "right" or "left." That person must then say the first and last name of the person sitting to his or her right or left before the person in the middle can say, "Bitty, Bitty, bum." If the person can't, he or she must move to the middle of the circle.

Continue the game until everyone has had a chance to try to introduce a person.

VARIATION

You can vary this game a little by yelling out: Name scramble! When you do, everyone in the circle should get up and move to a new spot. This added element will make sure the kids pay attention to everyone's name.

BLINDFOLDED SQUARE

Overview: Kids will build a square with rope while blindfolded.

Game Type: Discussion-starter, outside, senior high, suitable for disabled, team-builder

Group Size: Any

Time Involved: 10 to 20 minutes

Supplies: Blindfolds and a rope that's long enough for every group
member to have about a three-foot section

Preparation: None

Take the kids outside to a large open area. Have them form a circle and
put on blindfolds. Walk around the circle, hand each student a piece of rope,
and instruct kids to hold onto the rope until you give them further
instructions.

After everyone has a piece of rope, instruct the group to form a square
with straight sides using only their voices and tugs on the rope.

As the students try to work out a square, you can help lure them further
by asking questions such as "Who is leading, and who is following?" When
kids feel they have the best square possible, allow them to take off their
blindfolds and look at the square they formed.

This game can lead into a discussion about leadership and servanthood.
Using 1 Corinthians 9:19 and Galatians 5:13, discuss when it's better to be a
leader and when it's better to be a servant. Ask kids about their reaction to
the game, and allow those who were frustrated to express why they felt the
way they did. Ask:

- **What made this game difficult?**
- **How did "serving" one another assist in completing this square?**
- **How does this game reflect the Scriptures we read?**
- **How would this game function if everyone tried to be a leader? if
  everyone tried to be a servant? if some tried to be leaders and
  some tried to be servants?**

BLINDMAN'S DICTIONARY HUNT

Overview: Kids will help blindfolded teammates look up words in a dictionary.

Game Type: Discussion-starter, knowledge-builder, quiet, suitable for disabled, team-builder

Group Size: 20 to 30

Time Involved: 10 to 20 minutes

Supplies: Dictionaries, paper, pens, and blindfolds

Preparation: None

Have kids form teams of three, and distribute paper and pens. Tell teams to write three sentences about what it means to be a friend. Then walk around and circle three words in each team's sentences. Distribute dictionaries and blindfolds, and instruct each team to blindfold one team member. Explain that the blindfolded person will look up the circled words in the dictionary with a second person's help. The second person may not touch the dictionary; he or she may give only verbal cues.

When the blindfolded person has found the correct page, the third team member must write down the definition. Then they repeat the process until they've written down the definitions for the three words.

Start the game, and declare the first team to locate and write down the definitions the winner. When all teams have located their definitions, ask each team to read aloud its words and definitions. Use this game to begin a discussion about true friendship.

BODY-PART CHALLENGE

Overview: Kids will attempt to group themselves by various body parts.

Game Type: Funny, mixer, no supplies and no preparation, suitable for disabled

Group Size: 30 to 50

Time Involved: 2 to 10 minutes

Supplies: None

Preparation: None

Instruct the kids to move around the room. After a minute or so, call out a body part and a number—"Six noses," for example. Then kids must find five other people to touch noses with. Kids that don't respond quickly enough must sit out. Keep calling out various body parts and numbers until everyone is sitting out.

BREAKAWAY PUZZLERS

Overview: Kids will put together sayings about friendship.

Game Type: Quiet, suitable for disabled

Group Size: Any

Time Involved: 20 to 30 minutes

Supplies: Blank white cardboard puzzles (found in dollar stores and craft stores), markers, decorative stickers, and small plastic storage bags

Preparation: None

Have kids form teams of four, and give each team a blank puzzle. Distribute markers, stickers, and plastic bags. Ask each team to write on the puzzle a sentence about being a good friend or a saying about friendship. Have each team decorate its puzzle with markers and stickers before breaking apart the pieces and putting them into a plastic bag.

When teams are ready, have them exchange puzzles. When you say "go," have teams race to see which can put its puzzle together the fastest. As soon as each team completes a puzzle, team members should stand and read the saying aloud.

BUBBLE BUNS

Overview: Kids will try to transport a load of balloons without dropping them.

Game Type: Active, funny

Group Size: 30 to 50

Time Involved: 2 to 10 minutes

Supplies: One eleven-inch balloon for every person, with several more for backup

Preparation: None

Establish a starting line and a finish line, and have kids form teams of four to six. Give each person a balloon to inflate and tie off.

Have the first two players of each team stand back-to-back at the starting line and wedge two balloons between their bottoms while the other team members simply hold their balloons. The entire team must then walk to the finish line without dropping any balloons. When the team reaches the finish line, have three team members wedge three balloons between their bottoms. Then the entire team must walk back to the starting line, where they should add a fourth person and balloon. Continue until the team is transporting all their balloons without dropping any of them. The first team to carry all the balloons across the playing area wins.

BUILDING BLOCKS OF FRIENDSHIP

Overview: Kids will use ABC building blocks to form words describing friendship.

Game Type: Discussion-starter, suitable for disabled

Group Size: Any

Time Involved: 10 to 20 minutes

Supplies: A large assortment of ABC building blocks

Preparation: None

Have kids form teams of four or fewer. Distribute a variety of building blocks to each group. Instruct teams each to spell a word that describes a characteristic of friendship, what friendship means, or what a good friend is. Each team must stack its blocks vertically so the word they've chosen reads from top to bottom.

> ## LEADER TIP
>
> If no ABC building blocks are available, use Scrabble game pieces instead.

As soon as a team has completed a word, team members should shout it out. Then everyone else must stop and tear down the blocks they're working on. The team who formed the word first must support its word by giving reasons why that word relates to friendship. Continue the game for as long as time allows.

BUSY BUS

Overview: Kids will use body motions to take make-believe trips around the world.

Game Type: Funny, no supplies and no preparation, suitable for disabled

Group Size: 10 to 20

Time Involved: 20 to 30 minutes

Supplies: None

Preparation: None

Have kids sit on the floor as if sitting in a bus, with one person at the front as the "bus driver."

Say: **Each person will have the chance to be the driver. This person decides where the group is going by calling out monuments or landmarks from places around the world he or she has been. Designated objects may be famous or lesser known, but they should be real.**

As soon as an object is called, the two players seated closest to the driver work together to form the object and add sound effects when applicable. As the two players form the object, the other players must call out the city the object is in. If they're unable to do so, the driver must name another monument, and the game continues with the next players in line.

The game continues until someone guesses the location of the object. Then another driver gets a turn.

When someone correctly guesses the location, he or she gets one point. However if the driver "stumps" the group, he or she gets three points.

When everyone understands how to play, start the game. Have players keep track of their own scores, and play until everyone has been the driver. Then declare the person with the most points the winner.

Car-Wash Games

Overview: Kids will play various games during a car wash.

Game Type: Active, outside, suitable for disabled, team-builder, water

Group Size: Any

Time Involved: More than 1 hour

Supplies: Car wash supplies, pencils, a paper, and a watch

Preparation: Prepare as you regularly would for a car wash. The games themselves require no preparation.

Before the car wash, have kids form at least two teams. Each team should have no fewer than three members and no more than eight members. Explain that each team's members will work together and play together throughout the day. Tell kids that you'll keep a sheet of paper and a pencil at a central location and teams will be earning and keeping track of points throughout the car wash in these different ways:

• When a car drives up to get washed, the first team to correctly guess the make, model, and year of the car gets one point.

• When kids see the following cars anywhere in the vicinity and respond with the corresponding action, that team gets one point:

1. Volkswagen bug: Shout, "Slug bug!"

2. Mustang: Shout, "Giddy-up!"

3. Corvette: Shout, "Va-*room!*"

4. Cadillac: Shout, "Pass the Grey Poupon!"

• Have teams see which can wash a car the fastest. Teams can either wash different cars simultaneously, or you can use a watch and have teams wash alternate cars. The fastest team gets six points. However, each team may also name one person as a quality inspector. After a team washes a car, the inspector should quickly and fairly check the glass, tires, body, top, grill, and back bumper. For each area a team must redo, it loses one point. Encourage teams to develop strategies for the most efficient way to wash a car, and encourage quality inspectors to be fair. You may want to ask adult volunteers to fill in as quality inspectors. Be sure kids know that nobody expects perfection; teams shouldn't lose points because they're not perfect.

• During a lull, have two teams play this game. One team should line up in single file. This team should get a bucket of water and a sponge. The other team should line up in single file, starting about ten feet away, with another person at each additional five-foot point. The first person on the sponge-and-bucket team gets a chance to throw the sponge at the other team. If the first person on that team is hit, the team gets one point; if the second person is hit, the team gets two points, and so on. Be sure kids understand that a hard throw or a throw to the face is not OK. Each member of the first team should get a chance to throw the sponge, and then teams should switch roles.

At the end of the car wash, tally up the points. The team that loses has to clean up.

Cartoon Friends

Overview: Kids will answer a series of cartoon-related questions.

Game Type: Discussion-starter, icebreaker, suitable for disabled

Group Size: Any

Time Involved: 10 to 20 minutes

Supplies: Name tags, pens, and the "Cartoon Questions" handout (p. 131)

Preparation: Make photocopies of the "Cartoon Questions" handout (p. 131).

Have each person put on a name tag with his or her name and favorite cartoon character. Distribute "Cartoon Questions" handouts (p. 131), and have each person find someone else with the same character or a character from the same cartoon. Then have pairs write down their partners' responses to the questions on the handout. Afterward, have kids share with the group some of the responses.

Use this game to lead into a discussion about the biblical definition of happiness as found in Matthew 5:3-12.

Cartoon Questions

1. What is the first cartoon you remember watching?

2. If you could live in a perfect world, which cartoon world would you live in? Why?

3. What is the most admirable thing you can think of a cartoon character doing?

4. What was the happiest time in your life that was like a cartoon?

Celebrity Auction

Overview: Kids will take part in an auction to buy "celebrities'" items.

Game Type: Mixer, suitable for disabled

Group Size: 30 to 50

Time Involved: More than 1 hour

Supplies: The "Play Money" handout (p. 134), scissors, name tags, pens, newsprint, a marker, and the following items to be auctioned (or items that better fit your group):
- a letter signed by Abraham Lincoln,
- Babe Ruth's baseball uniform,
- a family Bible from the seventeenth century,
- a bag of peanuts grown on Jimmy Carter's family farm,
- a handwritten poem by Maya Angelou,
- a pair of Michael Jordan's athletic shoes,
- a pair of Jesus' sandals, and
- Dorothy's dress from *The Wizard of Oz.*

Preparation: Make photocopies of the "Play Money" handout (p. 134), and cut out the money. You'll need $50,000 of play money for every teenager. Place the items to be auctioned on a table. For each item, write on a slip of paper a number and what the item is. Then on a sheet of newsprint, write a corresponding numbered list of the items.

As each teenager arrives, give him or her $50,000 in play money. Have kids each put on a name tag, but write their favorite movie star's name on it. Instruct the kids to form pairs by matching names on name tags or by matching two movie stars who've starred in a movie together. Then tell pairs to combine their money because they will be co-bidders at an auction. Allow the kids to look over the items and discuss with their partners what they'd like and how much they're willing to pay.

To run the auction, hold up an item and flamboyantly describe it. Then begin the bidding at $1000, and encourage teenagers to shout out their bids. When the bidding slows, announce the final bid amount, and say: **Going once,**

LEADER TIP

For even more fun, turn this game into a party! Contact the kids in advance, and ask them to wear their fanciest clothes—prom dresses, fancy ties, and tacky and glitzy jewelry, for example. Ask an adult volunteer to act as a photographer to snap pictures of the kids as they arrive. Decorate the area with elegant tables, candles, and glitter. Create a banner that says "Celebrity Auction" to hang over the doorway. Prepare "fancy" snacks such as finger sandwiches.

going twice, sold! Then have the pair with the highest bid pay for the item. Continue until you auction off every item.

Afterward, discuss how pairs placed value on the items, which items were most important, and why those items were important. The discussion will help kids learn what's important to others in the group.

Play Money

CHAIR CARRY

Overview: Kids will carry chairs and place them in different positions.

Game Type: Active, discussion-starter, mixer

Group Size: Any

Time Involved: 10 to 20 minutes

Supplies: Chairs

Preparation: None

Have kids form teams of four to six. Gather all the teams in the center of the room where the game will begin. Explain that players will get better acquainted by helping each other carry chairs back and forth across the room.

Say: **A team will each transport its chair to the four corners of the room without bumping into another team along the way. If two or more teams touch, each must stop and set its chair on floor; then the entire team must sit on that chair as best as possible. Then the teams may continue. Also, only one team is allowed in a corner at a time.**

At each corner, set the chair in a different position—on its back, upside down, on its side, or at an angle, for example.

Explain that once the chair is in position, one team member must somehow sit on the chair and share the following information: full name, favorite dessert, and favorite sport or hobby. Encourage the other players to remember all the information.

Say: **When you're finished in one corner, carry your chair to another corner and listen to another player. Continue until all team members have shared; then move back to your starting position to show that you're finished.**

Start the game. When everyone has finished, have kids form new teams and play again. After several rounds, gather everyone together. Ask:

- Can anyone remember the information shared by members of his or her original team?
- Can anyone remember the information shared by members of every team on which he or she was a part?

- What might this game teach us about listening?
- What could we learn about making friends?

Say: **Sometimes we do not have very long to build lasting friend-ships. We may see someone only once. So we can make the most of any interaction with another person. Who knows, the next person you meet might turn out to be a best friend for life.**

CHARIOT RACE

Overview: Kids will use towels as chariots to carry team members to the head of the line.

Game Type: Active

Group Size: 20 to 30

Time Involved: 2 to 10 minutes

Supplies: Towels

Preparation: None

Have kids form two teams, and have each team form a single-file line. Give the first person in each line a towel.

Explain that at your signal, the first player in each line will pass the towel over his or her head to the next player. That player will then pass the towel overhead to the next player, and so on down the line.

Say: **When the towel reaches the last player in line, the two players just ahead in line will immediately drop back, grab the ends of the towel, and carry the person to the head of the line. Then the two carriers will rush to the back of the line. The player who has just been carried to the front will start passing the towel back overhead again.**

Start the game, and have teams play until everyone has been carried in the towel "chariot" and the original first player is back in position. The first team to finish wins the game.

CIRCLE SOCCER

Overview: Kids will use teamwork to move a soccer ball from one end of a room to the opposite end.

Game Type: Active, team-builder

Group Size: 20 to 30

Time Involved: 10 to 20 minutes

Supplies: A soccer ball

Preparation: None

Have the kids form a circle at one end of the room and hold hands. Drop a soccer ball in the middle of the circle, and inform the kids that they need to take the soccer ball to the other end of the room without dropping hands and without allowing the ball to leave the circle. When kids have moved the ball to the other end of the room, they've reached their goal.

VARIATION

Here are a few ways to change the game:

- If you have a large group, have them form teams and see which can successfully get across the room first.
- Time the group; then encourage them to try to beat their time.
- Instead of using one soccer ball, place two soccer balls in the circle.
- Use balloons instead of soccer balls.

CLIQUE BREAKDOWN

Overview: Kids will begin to recognize and combat cliques in the group.

Game Type: Active, discussion-starter, junior high, no supplies and no preparation, team-builder

Group Size: 10 to 20

Time Involved: 2 to 10 minutes

Supplies: None

Preparation: None

Have the entire group form a large circle and lock arms at the elbows so that the circle cannot be broken. Select one person to step outside the circle and attempt to break in through a locked elbow while the others try to keep him or her out.

Give several kids a chance to try to break into the circle. You might select the person with the first birthday of the year or the person who has lived in town the shortest length of time or the person with the longest last name to establish the point that often, when people are different, we do not let them into our group. Ask:

- How was this game like being in a clique?
- How did you feel when you were being kept out of the group?
- How did you feel when you were trying to keep others out?
- How can we prevent cliques from forming and remember to include everyone?

COKE OR PEPSI?

Overview: Kids will try to convince others that their drink is the best.

Game Type: Discussion-starter, icebreaker, suitable for disabled

Group Size: Any

Time Involved: 10 to 20 minutes

Supplies: A watch, a paper sack, a Coke, and a Pepsi

Preparation: Place the Coke and Pepsi in the paper sack.

Have kids form two sides based on their preference for either Coke or Pepsi. Inform the kids that they're going to try to convince someone on the other side that their favorite drink is the best drink in the world. Tell kids to use any means they can think of (except physical force) to convince the person to switch to their drink. At the end of the time limit, you will reveal which choice is the *right* choice.

Have kids approach those on the other side and try to convince them to switch brands. Time the activity, giving kids approximately five minutes to argue their case. You might remind them of the slogans and advertisements each drink uses. When time is up, gather everyone together. Ask:

- Did any of you want to switch drinks based on what the person said?
- What difficulties did you experience in this activity?
- When you're among your friends, how easy or difficult is it to make the right choice? Explain.
- Do you ever try to convince others that Jesus is the right choice for them?

Bring kids' attention to the paper sack. Pull one of the drinks out of the sack, and say:

Today someone may try to convince you that this drink is the right choice. Tomorrow the right choice may be the other drink. The world constantly changes what is the "right choice" based on what's popular. But it's good to know that God gave us Jesus so we can make the *true* right choice, a choice that will always be right.

COMMON GROUND

Overview: Kids will try to discover what they have in common with other group members.

Game Type: Mixer, quiet, suitable for disabled

Group Size: Any

Time Involved: 10 to 20 minutes

Supplies: Pencils, paper, and a watch

Preparation: None

Distribute one piece of paper and a pencil to each member of your group, and then say:

In this game, you'll try to discover what you have in common with the other members of the group.

Have kids create three columns on their papers: a "name" column, a "likes" column, and a "dislikes" column.

Say: **For the next fifteen minutes, walk around and find out both a like and a dislike that you have in common with another member of the group. When you have both discovered a common like and dislike and recorded that response, move on to another person. The goal is to get as many of these completed as you can. Make sure you find a different like and dislike for each person in the group you chat with.**

CRY, BABY, CRY

Overview: Kids will form pairs based on facial expressions and then talk to each other.

Game Type: Funny, icebreaker, mixer, no supplies and no preparation, suitable for disabled

Group Size: Any

Time Involved: 2 to 10 minutes

Supplies: None

Preparation: None

Gather kids together, and then ask them to walk around.

Say: **Keep walking around, but also make a face that conveys an emotion. For example, you could cry if you want to convey sadness, grin and laugh if you want to convey happiness, or narrow your eyes and purse your lips if you want to convey anger.**

Have kids form groups with one or two other people who are conveying the same emotion. Then ask group members to tell each other about a time they experienced that emotion.

Give kids a couple of minutes to share, and then have kids walk around again, make new faces, form new groups, and talk about experiences. Continue the same pattern for a couple more rounds.

DISK SURPRISE

Overview: Kids will write positive messages on computer disks and trade them.

Game Type: Affirmation, quiet, suitable for disabled, team-builder

Group Size: Any

Time Involved: More than 1 hour

Supplies: Computer disks and a marker

Preparation: Number the disks before the meeting, and write a group member's name by each number.

Give each teenager in your group the computer disk with his or her name written on it. Ask the kids to take the disks home and type a paragraph or two about why the group is special.

Then tell the kids to bring the disks back to the next meeting. Exchange the disks, making sure no one receives his or her own, and have the kids write again. Repeat this a few times so every person will help to build up the group by writing a few nice things. If you like, keep the disks and add new items throughout the year, making a kind of serial story of the youth group.

VARIATION

Use this activity as a personal affirmation activity by giving kids disks with other kids' names on them. Then have each person write something positive about the person whose name is on the disk. Have kids pass around the disks and add to the comments. Eventually, give kids the disks with their own names.

LEADER TIP

Group members who don't own computers may be able to borrow a friend's, a school's, or even the church's.

Don't Look Now—I'm Morphing

Overview: Kids will use their powers of observation to interact with each other.

Game Type: Discussion-starter, no supplies and no preparation, quiet, suitable for disabled, travel

Group Size: Any

Time Involved: 2 to 10 minutes

Supplies: None

Preparation: None

Have kids form pairs. Ideally, partners shouldn't know each other very well.

Say: **Now that you have a partner, I want you to take just a minute to observe and remember as much as you can about your partner's appearance.**

After about a minute, say:

Now I want each person to turn around, facing away from your partner. Without peeking at what your partner is doing, change five

things about your appearance. For example, comb your hair differently, remove or add glasses, and so on.

After you have given everyone a minute or two to make their changes, say:

Now turn back around and see if you can identify all the changes your partner made.

After another minute, ask the following questions:

- What was it like to stare at another person?
- What was it like for someone to stare at you?
- Was it difficult to change your appearance? Why or why not?

Lead kids into a discussion about how we present ourselves to others.

DUGOUTS

Overview: Kids will prepare a tasty snack together.

Game Type: Discussion-starter, food

Group Size: 2 to 10

Time Involved: 2 to 10 minutes

Supplies: Napkins, plastic knives, French bread, cheeses, sliced meats, and other deli items

Preparation: Place the items on a table.

The object of this game is for kids to work in teams to prepare Dugouts—French bread that has been hollowed in the center and filled with cheeses, meats and other deli items—and then consume them.

Have kids form teams of two or more. To begin, give each team an equal amount of ingredients and explain that the object of the game is to work together to hollow out the loaves of French bread, create a sandwich, and then work together to consume it. As kids work, create rules such as "You can't use your hands to make your sandwich" or "You must close your eyes while making the sandwich." Change the rules while kids are working.

As each team finishes its sandwich, have them eat their sandwiches with new rules, such as "You may not feed yourselves" and "You may not use your hands to eat."

Use this game to lead into a discussion about flexibility or how difficult it is to keep up with the world's changing "rules."

EAR-PULLING PARTY

Overview: Kids will play a gentle greeting game that breaks through shyness.

Game Type: Funny, icebreaker, no supplies and no preparation, suitable for disabled

Group Size: Any

Time Involved: 2 to 10 minutes

Supplies: None

Preparation: None

Have kids form a circle. Have one player start moving counterclockwise around the inside of the circle. This player should gently pull the ear of the person to his or her right and say "hello!" The ear-puller then should say his or her name, and the person whose ear was pulled should respond by saying his or her name. The ear-puller should move around the circle, greeting each person the same way.

As the ear-puller passes the person to his or her right, that person falls in behind the ear-puller and repeats the process with each person. Then the third person falls in behind the second, and so on. Soon, half of the circle is moving around.

As the first ear-puller completes the circle, he or she takes the original position and waits as the rest of the circle comes by in greeting.

THE EYES TELL ALL

Overview: Kids will look into each other's eyes and try to keep from laughing.

Game Type: Funny, no supplies and no preparation, suitable for disabled, travel

Group Size: Any

Time Involved: 2 to 10 minutes

Supplies: None

Preparation: None

Use this game to help kids become comfortable with one another or to break down any walls that have built up in your group. Have kids form two even groups, and have each group line up shoulder to shoulder and face the other group so that everyone has a partner. If you have an uneven number of students, join one of the lines so no one is without a partner.

Ask partners to hold hands and stare into one another's eyes without saying a word or laughing. Every ten seconds or so, say "switch," and have everyone move one spot to the right and face a new partner. The kids on the ends of the lines should simply move across into the other line.

After a few practice rounds, tell the students that anyone who talks or laughs will be out. Start the game, and continue until only two players are left. Allow the two to stare each other down until one person talks or laughs or looks away.

FAKE PILLOW FIGHT

Overview: Kids will encourage each other as you join this funny pillow fight.

Game Type: Active, funny

Group Size: 10 to 20

Time Involved: 2 to 10 minutes

Supplies: Three pillows, two blindfolds, and a watch

Preparation: None

Have kids form two teams, and have teams stand at opposite ends of the room. Blindfold the first player from each team, and give him or her a pillow. Explain that the object of the game is to see who can score the most pillow hits to his or her opponent in one minute. Have the blindfolded players start walking toward each other.

The catch to this game is that you are also equipped with a pillow, which you should use to alternately hit the players. This will confuse the players as to the location of the actual opponent, and only pillow hits to an actual opponent count.

Encourage teams to call out encouragement and directions to their players, and see which team has the highest total of hits after everyone has played.

FAMOUS YOU

Overview: Kids will attempt to introduce a friend as a famous look-alike.

Game Type: Funny, no supplies and no preparation, suitable for disabled, travel

Group Size: 2 to 10

Time Involved: 20 to 30 minutes

Supplies: None

Preparation: None

Have kids form pairs, and say:

It seems like everyone looks at least a little bit like someone famous. For this game, I'd like for each of you to think of a famous person who resembles your partner. This famous person can be alive or deceased, young or old, male or female.

Give kids a few minutes to think, and then have pairs take turns introducing their "famous" partners to the rest of the group by answering yes-or-no questions about their partners. Be sure kids ask only yes-or-no questions, such as "Are you alive?" "Are you a musician?" and "Are you in politics?"

Have kids play until the group guesses who each person resembles.

FOLD THE LINE

Overview: Kids will line up and then fold the line to meet someone face to face.

Game Type: Icebreaker, no supplies and no preparation, suitable for disabled

Group Size: Any

Time Involved: 2 to 10 minutes

Supplies: None

Preparation: None

Have students line up shoulder to shoulder according to hair color, from darkest to lightest. Have kids link arms and then fold the line exactly in half so kids end up facing each other. If you have an uneven number of kids, join the line yourself. Direct students each to say hello to the person they meet face to face and answer these three questions:

- **When is your birthday?**
- **What do you like best about school?**
- **What do you like best about God?**

Have the kids repeat the process at least three times, each time lining up by different criterion, such as by clothing colors or in alphabetical order. Ask different questions each time. Here are some possibilities:

- **What are the names of the people who live in your house?**
- **How long have you been coming to this church?**
- **What do you like to do in your free time?**
- **Who is your favorite Christian musician?**

FRAGILE FOOTBALL

Overview: Kids will move hollow-egg footballs down a "field."

Game Type: Funny, suitable for disabled

Group Size: 10 to 20

Time Involved: 2 to 10 minutes

Supplies: Newsprint, tape, a marker, an egg or a Ping-Pong ball, paper, pens, and a coin

Preparation: Cover a table with newsprint, and tape the newsprint securely to the underside of the table. Then draw the lines of a football field on the newsprint. To make the fragile football, use a pen or other point to punch two small holes in either end of an egg; blow into one end of the egg to force the contents out the other end. Then draw markings on the egg to resemble a football. Make several extra "footballs."

Have kids form two teams, and have teams gather at opposite ends of the prepared table. Give each team a sheet of paper and a pen to use to keep score. Have teams each choose a captain, and let captains participate in a coin toss to determine which team starts.

Have the first person on the team that wins the coin toss place the egg on his or her team's goal line. Then have the player take a big breath and see how far he or she can blow the egg down the "field." Players must hold their hands behind their backs during play. Award the team points based on where the egg stops. For example, if the egg stops near the player's thirty-yard line, the team receives thirty points. If the egg stops near the opponents' thirty-yard line, the team receives seventy points.

If the egg goes out of bounds, the points are determined from the point at which the egg went out. If the egg goes all the way down the field and across the opposing team's goal line, the team gets one hundred points. The team with the highest score after all players have had a turn wins.

VARIATION

Have all team members play at once, with opposing teams each trying to blow the egg into the other team's territory. Use a whistle to time each play at thirty seconds, and record the score after each time out.

FRIENDSHIP COOPERATION

Overview: Kids will discover the art of cooperating with a friend.

Game Type: Active, discussion-starter, suitable for disabled, team-builder

Group Size: Any

Time Involved: 30 to 45 minutes

Supplies: Paper, a pen, and a watch

Preparation: Create a list of tasks that must be accomplished to win the game. You'll need one list for each pair of players. Here are some examples for a camping or retreat setting:
- Go to your cabin and make your bed.
- Gather ten pieces of kindling for a fire, and bring them back to the campfire ring.
- Wash your face in the stream.
- Do ten jumping jacks.
- Make a cross using only things found in nature.

Have kids form pairs. Each pair should lock right arms at the elbows so that the partners are facing opposite directions. Give each pair a list of tasks to complete to win the game, and tell them they have thirty minutes. Remind kids that they must keep their arms hooked the entire time and return within thirty minutes.

After thirty minutes, when everyone has returned, say:

It's often difficult to be friends. Sometimes it's hard to agree or cooperate.

Ask:

- **Did you sometimes find it difficult to agree with your partner?**
- **What did you have to do to successfully complete your tasks?**

FRIENDSHIP FORGIVENESS

Overview: Kids will explore the art of forgiveness and its relationship to healthy friendships.

Game Type: Discussion-starter, quiet, suitable for disabled

Group Size: 2 to 10

Time Involved: 10 to 20 minutes

Supplies: Containers of soap bubbles and bubble wands

Preparation: None

Have kids form pairs, and give each pair a container of bubbles. Explain that they're going to tell each other about a time a friend hurt them or upset them; as they talk, they'll blow a bubble. The partner will suggest one way to forgive that person and will then pop the bubble.

Have kids play and switch roles after about five minutes.

When everyone has had a chance to share, call them together again. Ask volunteers to share what they learned about forgiveness. Ask:

- **How was popping the bubbles like forgiving someone?**
- **How can we help each other forgive?**

FRIENDSHIP KEEPERS

Overview: Kids will identify biblical principles for friendship.

Game Type: Bible, discussion-starter, mixer, quiet, suitable for disabled

Group Size: 20 to 30

Time Involved: 2 to 10 minutes

Supplies: Bibles, concordances, newsprint, tape, and markers

Preparation: Tape newsprint—one sheet per team—on a wall, and place a Bible, concordance, and marker on the floor in front of each sheet of newsprint.

Have kids form teams of four and line up at the opposite end of the room from the newsprint. Tell the kids they're going to explore ways to maintain friendships.

Say: **When I say "go," the first person from each team will run to the concordance, look up the word "friend," look up a Scripture reference, and write on the newsprint one thought that Scripture says about friendship. Then he or she will run back and tag the next team member, who'll repeat the process. The first team to finish wins.**

Start the game. When teams are finished, follow up with a discussion around the passages and thoughts kids wrote. Be sure to give kids the opportunity to discuss their own experiences with friendship in conjunction with the Bible passages.

FRIENDSHIP WEB

Overview: Kids will create a web with yarn while learning names.

Game Type: Active, discussion-starter, suitable for disabled

Group Size: 20 to 30

Time Involved: 10 to 20 minutes

Supplies: A large ball of colored yarn

Preparation: None

Have kids sit in a circle. Then have each person around the circle loudly say his or her first name, and encourage everyone to pay close attention. As kids say their names, have the group loudly reply, "Welcome, [name]!"

After all the kids have introduced themselves, announce that they'll introduce themselves again. This time when they say their names, they'll also say their favorite junk food. For example, someone might say, "My name is Helen, and I like potato chips." The group then will respond, "Welcome, Helen. You like potato chips."

LEADER TIP

For best results, have the first person tossing the yarn tie it to his or her wrist first.

When kids have completed the second introduction, hold up a ball of yarn. Explain that kids will call out either the name or the junk food of any person across the circle and then will toss the ball of yarn to that person. However, they must hold onto the yarn as they toss it, preferably looping it around the wrist first.

After the second person catches the yarn, he or she should tighten it, loop it around a wrist, and call out another person's name or favorite junk food. Kids who are identified by their favorite junk food should call out their first names before they throw the yarn to someone else, and kids who are identified by their first names should call out their favorite junk food first.

Have kids repeat the process, each time tossing the yarn to someone new. If kids can't remember anyone's name or junk food, have someone on the opposite side of the circle volunteer his or her name and junk food again. Keep the game moving; continue until everyone has caught the yarn.

After the game, ask the group to look carefully at the yarn design they made. Point out that it resembles a large web, and then ask discussion questions such as the following:

- **How is this web design like friendship?**
- **What's it like to be part of this web? part of our group?**

Allow plenty of time for responses so everyone who wants to can answer.

GIBBER JABBER

Overview: Kids will teach others how to play games without using any known language.

Game Type: Discussion-starter, funny, no supplies and no preparation, suitable for disabled

Group Size: Any

Time Involved: 20 to 30 minutes

Supplies: None

Preparation: None

Ask group members to think privately of a game they want the group to play. Then ask for a volunteer to lead the group in playing his or her game. The catch is that neither the volunteer nor the rest of the group can use any known language.

Allow the first volunteer to try to explain his or her game. When the group figures out what the game is, have them play the game without speaking a known language. Then repeat the process with several other volunteers.

Use this game to lead into a discussion on how newcomers may feel when they come to your group or how non-Christians may feel when they attend a Christian church service or youth meeting. Begin the discussion with questions similar to the following:

- What was it like trying to explain your game to the rest of the group?
- What was it like trying to understand what was being explained?
- How were your feelings during the game similar to those newcomers or non-Christians may feel when they attend our group or church?
- How can we help new people feel more comfortable?

GIVE ME A KISS!

Overview: Kids will learn about others by asking yes-or-no questions and exchanging kisses—the chocolate kind.

Game Type: Funny, icebreaker, mixer, suitable for disabled

Group Size: Any

Time Involved: 10 to 20 minutes

Supplies: Chocolate kisses, paper, and a pen

Preparation: Create a list of yes-or-no questions that can help kids get to know one another, and then photocopy the list.

Say: **Paul wrote that Christians were to greet one another with a "holy kiss"** (1 Corinthians 16:20; 2 Corinthians 13:12), **so that's what you'll do in this game.**

Distribute photocopies of the questions you prepared. Explain that kids will each receive five *chocolate* kisses with which to play the game.

Say: **You'll walk around the room and ask each other questions. If player 1 asks player 2 a question and player 2 responds with a "yes," player 2 has to give player 1 a kiss. If player 2 says "no," no kisses change hands. You can't ask anyone more than one question. When you run out of kisses, sit down. The object of the game is to end up with the most kisses.**

You may want to put a time limit on the game, too—from three to five minutes.

Distribute the chocolate kisses, and begin the game. At the end of the allotted time, declare the person with the most kisses the "kissing champion."

GOURMET COOKIE CREATIONS

Overview: Kids will create "gourmet" cookie creations to share.

Game Type: Food, suitable for disabled

Group Size: 10 to 20

Time Involved: 10 to 20 minutes

Supplies: Paper plates, an assortment of small cookies, cans of whipped cream, cherries, plastic knives and spoons, and napkins

Preparation: Set the supplies on a table.

Have kids form groups of three or four, and give each group a paper plate, an assortment of six to eight cookies, a can of whipped cream, and cherries. Have groups create gourmet cookie creations for everyone to enjoy. Remind groups to pay attention to color, texture, presentation, and height. You may also want to give kids a time limit.

If you like, judge the final results, or have kids judge the creations before consuming the evidence.

GROUP SCRAPBOOKS

Overview: Kids will create books about group members and hobbies.

Game Type: Icebreaker, suitable for disabled

Group Size: 20 to 30

Time Involved: 30 to 45 minutes

Supplies: Polaroid cameras with film, paper, glue, staplers, and pens

Preparation: None

Have kids form groups of four or five. Within those groups, have kids take turns photographing each other doing things they like to do. For example, they could pose with a basketball or a book.

When kids have finished taking the pictures, have them glue the pictures to sheets of paper and write a couple of sentences about each picture and person. Then have each group staple the sheets of paper together to create a book.

When groups have finished making the books, have them share the books with everyone by reading them aloud.

GUMSHOE INTERVIEWS

Overview: Kids will interview one another's shoes.

Game Type: Funny, icebreaker, suitable for disabled

Group Size: 20 to 30

Time Involved: 30 to 45 minutes

Supplies: Pens and paper

Preparation: None

Distribute small pieces of paper, and have kids write their names on the papers. Then ask kids to remove their shoes and place the papers inside. Explain that the word "gumshoe" is slang for a detective and that kids are going to play gumshoes to figure out who each pair of shoes belongs to.

Place several pairs of shoes several feet apart from each other in a row. Using the names placed in the shoes, select a gumshoe for each pair of shoes. Avoid placing a gumshoe with his or her own shoes or a good friend's shoes, and be sure to remove the name from the shoe. Have the gumshoes face the shoes, and then ask the shoes' owners to stand behind the gumshoes. Inform kids that at no time may a gumshoe turn to face the shoes' owner or in any way be informed who owns the shoes.

Have the gumshoes interview the shoes for five minutes, asking questions to help identify the shoes' owners. When the owners respond, they should be as evasive as possible, by using misleading, confusing, or distracting answers. However, at no time may the owners lie; if they do, the gumshoes win by default. Owners may also disguise their voices, speak in fake accents, and so on, to further confuse the gumshoes.

Repeat this process until everyone has been both an owner and a gumshoe. Then have everyone gather together again. Pair by pair, set the shoes before the group. Ask the gumshoe who interviewed each pair name who he or she thinks is the owner of the shoes and why. If the gumshoes guess correctly, they win. If they don't guess correctly, the owners win.

HAPPY FEET

Overview: Girls will ask guys get-acquainted questions, and guys will respond with funny foot movements while hidden from view.

Game Type: Funny, icebreaker, senior high, suitable for disabled

Group Size: 30 to 50

Time Involved: 30 to 45 minutes

Supplies: Two or three large blankets, safety pins, strong string, paper, a marker, five stools or a long bench, and the "Interview Questions" handout (p. 157) or another list of suggested questions

Preparation: Section off a part of the room by hanging blankets with string. Leave a gap of about twelve inches between the bottom of the blankets and the floor. Position the stools or the bench behind the blankets, and pin five sheets of paper across the front of the blankets, one in front of each stool. On the sheets of paper, number the positions from one to five. Photocopy the "Interview Questions" handout (p. 157), or prepare questions appropriate for your group.

This is a great game to play at the beginning of a dance or party, but it works best with an equal number of guys and girls.

Take the girls out of the room while the guys remove their shoes and socks and roll up their pant legs. Place five guys behind the blankets, and have the rest of the guys wait out of sight in another area.

Bring in five girls at a time, and give them an "Interview Questions" handout (p. 157). Have them each take a turn asking the guys a couple of

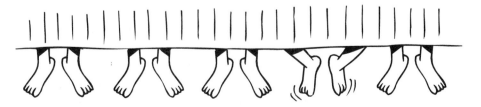

LEADER TIP

Before the game begins, you may want to give the guys some fun ideas about their foot movements. For example, if they want to respond with an enthusiastic "yes," they can slap the bottoms of their feet together like a happy seal. Or if they're puzzled by a question, they can slowly scratch one foot with the other foot. If they're shocked, they can stomp on the floor and then jerk their feet up and out of sight behind the blankets. Urge the guys to use their imaginations and have fun.

questions. Let each guy respond, but here's the catch: The guys can only respond with their feet. They may stomp, kick, sway, and do anything else to answer with their feet.

If the girls don't understand the meaning of the foot movements, they may ask the guys for clarity, but the guys may never speak. They may only try to clarify with more foot movements.

At the end of each five-minute interview period, have the girls select the guys by number. Because the last girl and guy are paired by a process of elimination, encourage everyone to applaud the last couple for being good sports. Then have the kids introduce themselves to their partners and move to the back of the room to enjoy the rest of the interviews.

Have the girls who are waiting to interview the guys add their own questions to the list, creating questions appropriate to the occasion or to the group. Allow each group of five girls five minutes to interview the guys. Keep the interviewing process moving along! Continue bringing in five girls and five guys until everyone has a partner.

 # Interview Questions

1. Number _____, if I select you, can I paint your toenails with firetruck-red nail polish?

2. Number _____, is there a TV family like your family?

3. Number _____, do you have a home page on the Internet?

4. Number _____, are you a Bulls fan?

5. Number _____, do you have a cat?

6. Number _____, do you like to laugh a lot?

7. Number _____, if I select you, will you sing me a song?

8. Number _____, did you use deodorant today?

9. Number _____, do you like tall girls?

10. Number _____, are you better looking than the guys beside you?

11. Number _____, would it bother you if I were a better basketball player than you?

12. Number _____, do you like picnics in the park?

13. Number _____, do you like cold pieces of leftover pizza?

14. Number _____, would you wear one of my rings in your nose if I selected you?

15. Number_____, would you talk to me if I had green hair and purple lips?

16. Number_____, do you have belly-button lint?

17. Number_____, do you like country songs and twangy guitar music?

18. Number_____, do you have any beanie babies?

19. Number _____, do you cry during sad movies?

20. Number _____, do you sleep with a stuffed animal?

Hey, Buddy, Can You Spare a Dime?

Overview: Kids will don sticky hats and collect items on their heads.

Game Type: Active, discussion-starter, funny, senior high, suitable for disabled

Group Size: Any

Time Involved: 45 to 60 minutes

Supplies: Nylon hose, scissors, duct tape, and stocking caps. You may also need additional supplies as described below.

Preparation: Cut off the legs of several pairs of hose; one leg for each player. Then cut a small circle out of each leg so when a player puts the hose on his or her head, the hole leaves room for the face.

Careful preparation is *very* important in this game. Have each player put a nylon-hose leg over his or her head to cover the hair. Then place a stocking cap on the head of any player who has long hair. These are *not* steps to skip unless you want all your kids to shave their heads.

Unroll duct tape and, with the sticky side *out,* create a cap that fits on each player's head. Run a piece of duct tape (still facing out) under the player's chin to connect both sides of the cap and keep it in place. Now each player has a dull silver sticky cap that's just perfect for collecting loose change.

Depending on what's legal in your town and how much time you have, have your kids do one of the following activities:

- Place kids in a public environment where they can ask passersby for spare change. Use the money for a ministry project.
- Send kids to the homes of church members to ask for money, pins, nails, Ping-Pong balls, or other objects that will stick well to their caps. (This makes for a *memorable* scavenger hunt.)
- Have kids form teams and play catch using dimes or balloons. The object is to toss objects and see if team members can catch them by positioning their heads under them. (Caution: To avoid head-to-head collisions, do this in pairs *only.*)

After the game, be sure to give adequate time for discussion. Have kids form trios and *carefully* remove their caps. Ask them to help each other with this procedure. Then ask trios to discuss the following questions:

- **How did people react to you? Why?**
- **How did you feel during this game?**
- **What was one memorable moment for you? Why?**
- **How was this experience like and unlike being physically disabled in an obvious way?**

Hot Buttons

Overview: Kids will make creative name tags to affirm each other.

Game Type: Affirmation, mixer, suitable for disabled

Group Size: Any

Time Involved: 2 to 10 minutes

Supplies: Slips of paper, a pen, a hat or bag, name tags, and colorful markers

Preparation: Write each group member's name on a slip of paper, and place the slips in a hat or bag.

Have each group member secretly draw a name from the hat. Inform kids that they'll be making name tags for the people whose names they drew. First, though, they each must interview three group members about that person without letting that person know. Then kids each must create a name tag that illustrates or describes several of that person's positive qualities. No one's name should actually appear on a name tag.

After kids have finished, have them hold up the name tags, walk around the room, and look at all the name tags to try to find their own. When they think they've found their own name tags, they must ask the person holding it up if it's theirs. That person may respond only by nodding or shaking his or her head. When kids find their name tags, the people who created them must explain why they included what they did.

Have kids wear their name tags for the rest of the meeting.

How We See Ourselves

Overview: Kids will compare how they see themselves with how others see them.

Game Type: Discussion-starter, quiet, senior high, suitable for disabled

Group Size: 10 to 20

Time Involved: 20 to 30 minutes

Supplies: Paper, pens, and a large hat or paper bag

Preparation: None

Have kids sit in a circle; distribute paper and pens. Instruct players each to write down—in one sentence—a positive attribute or that makes them special. Have them write their names next to their attributes and then pass papers to you. Place the papers in a hat.

Randomly draw the papers from the hat, read aloud each attribute, and have everyone guess the name of the person the attribute belongs to. Allow three or four guesses before revealing the name.

Afterward, have kids discuss how the way they see themselves differs from the way others see them. For example, some people assume things about us without getting to know us. And we might consider new and more demonstrative ways to share our attributes with others. Emphasize that God knows us completely and delights in the attributes he has given us.

How Do You Do?

Overview: Kids will become better acquainted by assigning a different connecting body part for each name.

Game Type: Mixer, suitable for disabled

Group Size: 20 to 30

Time Involved: 2 to 10 minutes

Supplies: A watch

Preparation: None

Explain that kids will have three minutes to meet everyone in the room. Add that as players greet one another, they are to do variations of the handshake, such as elbow rubs or foot slaps. The catch is that players may not use the same body part twice. For example, if player 1 and player 2 shake hands, they can't shake hands with anyone else; if player 1 and player 3 rub elbows, they can't rub elbows with anyone else. Encourage players to be creative, but keep it clean.

When kids have greeted each other, see who can correctly match the name and motion used with every person in the room.

Hug Races

Overview: Kids will race and embrace.

Game Type: Active, funny, no supplies and no preparation, team-builder

Group Size: 30 to 50

Time Involved: 2 to 10 minutes

Supplies: None

Preparation: None

Have kids form teams of five and line up to run a relay. Have two team members from each team hug; then have the last three gather around them in a

VARIATION

Have teams hunt for a "treasure" while hugging to convey that kids must work together to accomplish the task.

hug. Explain that the object of this game is to race to a designated point while embracing and that the first team to do so wins. Start the race, and may the best hug win!

Human Hoop-Loops

Overview: Kids will move across a playing area in hoop-size increments.

Game Type: Active

Group Size: Any

Time Involved: 2 to 10 minutes

Supplies: Plastic hoops, such as Hula Hoops

Preparation: None

Have kids form trios, and place a plastic hoop in front of each trio. To move across the playing area, player 1 must step into the hoop. Player 2 must move in front of player 1 and lift the hoop up over player 1's body without letting the hoop touch player 1. Player 3 must move in front of player 2. Then player 2 must place the hoop over player 3's head and down to the ground without letting the hoop touch him or her. Player 1 must move in front of player 3, raise the hoop off player 3, and bring it over player 2 so that the trio is proceeding down the playing area.

To add to the friend-making experience, players may say something they like while lifting the hoop and something they dislike while placing the hoop onto the next player.

HUMAN PINBALL

Overview: Kids will play "pinball" with a twist.

Game Type: Active, outside

Group Size: 50 to 75

Time Involved: 10 to 20 minutes

Supplies: Blindfolds

Preparation: None

Have kids form teams of fifteen, and have each team spread out on the playing field so there are four rows about four feet apart. In the first row, two kids should stand about four feet apart. In the second row, three kids should stand about four feet apart. In the third row, four kids should stand about four feet apart. And in the fourth row, five kids should stand about four feet apart. Explain that the last person on each team will be the "pinball."

Say: **From now on, everyone must be completely silent.**

Blindfold each pinball, and lead him or her to stand somewhere between the third and fourth rows of the team. Spin each pinball several times, and then say:

The goal is for your pinball to walk through the "goal" (between the

two people in the first row). No one may talk, but if your pinball is going to bump into you, you can try to spin him or her toward the right direction. You can touch only your pinball's arms or shoulders, and only for one second. If you touch your pinball anywhere else or for longer than one second, he or she has to start from the beginning.

When everyone understands, begin the game. The team whose pinball finishes first wins. Have teams switch roles and play again.

Ice-Melting Contest

Overview: Kids will work with friends to melt blocks of ice.

Game Type: Funny, outside, suitable for disabled

Group Size: 2 to 10

Time Involved: 2 to 10 minutes

Supplies: A scale and ten-pound blocks of ice

Preparation: None

Have kids form pairs, and give each pair a block of ice. Weigh each pair's block of ice, and then tell kids they must melt as much of the block as possible without using fire, water, chipping or smashing; they may use only their breath.

Let kids try to melt the ice for about five to ten minutes. Then weigh each block. The pair with the lightest block wins the "hot air" award.

Imaginary Bowling

Overview: Kids will take turns rolling an imaginary bowling ball.

Game Type: Funny, suitable for disabled

Group Size: 2 to 10

Time Involved: 2 to 10 minutes

Supplies: Index cards, a marker, and masking tape

Preparation: For each player, make a set of four index cards, each marked with a 7, 8, 9, or 10.

Admit it: The best part of going bowling is watching how bowlers wind up and zing a pin-busting ball down the alley. Some bowlers move with almost poetic grace and style. Others throw or bounce the ball as if they're tossing a grenade.

Here's your group's chance to show their stuff without having to actually *go* to a bowling alley to rent silly-looking shoes—or keep score.

Create a line by placing a length of tape on the floor. Ask everyone to sit on one side of the line and face the line where the bowling pins usually sit. Give each person a set of four index cards. Ask everyone to take a turn walking to the other side of the line and approaching it in their best form as if they were rolling a bowling ball.

Have kids use their index cards to rate the style of the delivery, selecting any number from 7 to 10.

- A 7 indicates that the delivery was effective, attractive, and done with a fair degree of flair.
- An 8 indicates that the delivery was even better, one that showed pizazz.
- A 9 indicates that the delivery was approaching perfection, an art form in motion.
- A perfect 10 is the highest possible honor, indicating that the delivery was unique, masterful, the stuff of legend.

When everyone has had a turn, turn up the heat a notch by having kids form pairs for *tag team* bowling.

Jump-Rope Jive

Overview: Kids will jump rope while telling about themselves.

Game Type: Active, junior high

Group Size: Any

Time Involved: 2 to 10 minutes

Supplies: Jump-ropes

Preparation: None

Have kids get into several equal-numbered groups of at least three and no more than six, and give each group a jump-rope.

Say: **We're going to play a game in which you have to think fast on your feet. Two people will hold and turn the jump-rope, and then** everyone will take a turn jumping rope. Each time you jump over the rope, you must tell your group members something about yourself. For example, you might want to say your name, your birthday, your favorite color, and so on. We'll see who can jump and jive the longest!

Have kids take turns holding the rope so everyone gets a chance to jump. Then have kids form new groups and jump again until time's up.

Key Personalities

Overview: Kids will examine key chains to learn about each other.

Game Type: Icebreaker, no supplies and no preparation, senior high, suitable for disabled

Group Size: 2 to 10

Time Involved: 10 to 20 minutes

Supplies: None

Preparation: None

Have kids drop their key chains into a pile. To introduce the game, explain that kids will play a team of archaeologists who need to examine the objects to discover not their use, but the personality of their owners. For example, what do the number of keys, the type of keys, and the key chain trinkets tell us about the owners? Encourage the "archeologists" to look at the items from the perspective of someone thousands of years in the future.

Give each person a chance to close his or her eyes, draw a set of keys from the pile, and explain what the keys say about the owner. Encourage imagination, discussion, and maybe even a little debate. Since no answer is wrong, encourage everyone to share an opinion.

Knot Now!

Overview: Kids will race to see which team can unravel a string of knots faster.

Game Type: Active

Group Size: 10 to 20

Time Involved: 10 to 20 minutes

Supplies: Two strings or cords, each the length of the room

Preparation: Along each string, tie half the number of knots as there are kids in your group. The knots should be a similar type and should be tied fairly tightly.

Have kids form two teams, and have teams line up at one end of the room. Secure the strings to a table or chair leg at the opposite end of the room, and then stretch the strings across the room toward the teams.

At your signal, have the first player from each team run to the team's string, untie the first knot, then hurry back to tag the next player in line. The next player will untie the next knot, and so on until one team wins by untying all of its knots first.

LET IT SNOW!

Overview: Kids will love this collection of game ideas for a snowy day.

Game Type: Active, outside, suitable for disabled, winter

Group Size: Any

Time Involved: 30 to 45 minutes

Supplies: A snowy day, plastic trash can lids, and empty coffee cans or small buckets

Preparation: None

Use the following collection of games to bring out the little kids in your kids on a snowy day.

- **Target Practice**—Kids will test their ability to hit a target using snowballs. Have kids form two teams. Draw two large circles in the snow, and have each team stand fifteen feet away from its circle. At your signal, kids will quickly make snowballs and try to toss them gently into their circles. At the end of five minutes, see which team has the most snowballs inside its circle. (Broken snowballs don't count.)
- **Step Right Up**—Have kids line up about five feet away from a set of

steps. Let kids try to aim and hit each step in succession with a snowball.

- **Snowball Shields**—In this old-fashioned snowball fight, let teams use plastic trash can lids to shield themselves from the opposing team's snowball assault. Depending on how many lids you have, let kids try to infiltrate "enemy territory" either individually or circled around a teammate they're trying to protect. Teams take turns trying to reach a goal in the opposing team's area without getting hit by a snowball.
- **Fort-itude**—Have teams see who can build the biggest snow fort in five minutes. Give each team a collection of empty coffee cans or small plastic buckets to use as molds.

LIFTED UP

Overview: Kids will carry balloons through mazes in teams.

Game Type: Active, affirmation, discussion-starter, suitable for disabled, team-builder

Group Size: 10 to 20

Time Involved: 10 to 20 minutes

Supplies: Eleven-inch balloons (a bigger size is even better), slips of paper, and pencils

Preparation: Set up several mazes of chairs that stretch across the floor, one maze for each team of four or five kids.

Have kids form teams of four or five. Give each person a pencil and slip of paper. Ask team members to think about an affirmation they could use to describe each person in the group. Then have team members take turns telling each other the words. As each person hears the compliments, he or she should write the words on a slip of paper.

When teams have completed their slips of paper, give each a balloon. Tell teams to roll up their slips of paper, put them into the balloon, and then blow up the balloon.

Have each team line up behind its maze of chairs.

Say: **On my signal, you'll lock your arms in a tight team circle. Someone will throw your balloon into the air. Your team must keep the balloon in the air and move it and your team through the maze of chairs to the finish line. If your balloon touches the floor, you have to go back to the starting line and begin again. You cannot touch the balloon with your hands, and your arms must stay locked together.**

VARIATION
You can also give each person a balloon and have teams try to keep all the balloons in the air while they run the maze.

Start the race, and see which team gets its balloon over the finish line. After the game, have teams discuss these questions:

- What was it like to hear the positive things your team members said about you?
- What was difficult about keeping the balloon in the air while walking through a maze with your arms locked?
- How did you overcome the difficulties in the game?
- How can we keep each other "up" and overcome some of the difficulties we face as a group?

LOCATION, LOCATION, LOCATION

Overview: Kids will form pairs based on their ideal vacation destinations.

Game Type: No supplies and no preparation, quiet, suitable for disabled

Group Size: Any

Time Involved: 2 to 10 minutes

Supplies: None

Preparation: None

Use this game to help kids randomly form pairs.
Ask kids to stand and gather in the center of the room.

Say: **I want you to think of your ideal vacation destination. Money is no object. You have all the time you need to get there and get home. It can be a ski lodge in Aspen or a coral reef where you're scuba diving. Be as specific as possible as you think of the place you'd most like to** go on vacation right now, but don't tell anyone where it is! You have twenty seconds to form a picture of that place in your mind.

After about twenty seconds, say:

If the place you're thinking of is on land, move two steps to your left. If it's on or in water, move two steps to your right.

Wait for the migration to finish, and then continue:

If the place you're thinking of is above the equator, raise your right hand. If the place you're thinking of is below the equator, put your right hand at your side.

If you're imagining a lot of physical activity, raise your left hand. If you're imagining yourself relaxing, put your left hand by your side.

If getting to your ideal vacation destination requires flying, stand on your tiptoes. If it doesn't, stand normally.

If getting to your ideal vacation destination requires that you travel on water, quack like a duck. If not, say nothing.

Now find someone who's configured like yourself, pair up, and compare notes. Find out that person's ideal vacation destination!

MARBLE MATCHING

Overview: Kids will win marbles by matching descriptions to group members.

Game Type: Affirmation, suitable for disabled

Group Size: 10 to 20

Time Involved: 10 to 20 minutes

Supplies: Index cards, a pen, and marbles

Preparation: On index cards, write a short clue about each person in your group. Be sensitive when writing these clues; avoid naming physical or character traits that could embarrass someone. Instead, write neutral clues and an affirmation for each person. For example, *don't* write, "This person has flaming red hair and is a real bookworm," but *do* write, "This person has two brothers, two cats, and is always willing to help others study."

Have kids form two teams. Ask kids to take turns selecting a card and reading the card aloud. Both teams can begin calling out their guesses. The first team to correctly name the person gets one marble. Continue playing until all the cards are used. The team with the most marbles wins.

MEMORY MATCHES

Overview: Kids will try to find index card pairs.

Game Type: Icebreaker, quiet, senior high, suitable for disabled

Group Size: 2 to 10

Time Involved: 20 to 30 minutes

Supplies: Sixty to eighty index cards and pens

Preparation: Write "getting to know you" questions on the backs of the index cards, and make sure you write each question on two index cards.

Lay down all the cards with the questions facing down. Have kids take turns picking up a card, reading the question, answering it, and keeping it. When someone draws a card that matches one he or she already has, have that person keep both cards and take another turn. Continue until kids have matched all the cards. The player with the most cards wins.

MISSION MINDED

Overview: Kids will find Scriptures that describe how to share faith with others.

Game Type: Bible, discussion-starter, quiet, senior high, suitable for disabled

Group Size: 2 to 10

Time Involved: 20 to 30 minutes

Supplies: Bibles

Preparation: None

Have kids form two groups; distribute Bibles. Ask kids to find Scriptures about sharing faith. For example, in Acts 1:8 Jesus tells the disciples they'll be his "witnesses in Jerusalem, and in all Judea and Samaria, and to the ends of the earth." In response to each Scripture, ask kids to describe a time they've followed that Scripture. The first team to locate five verses that they've all followed in life wins.

Afterward, lead kids into a discussion about sharing faith.

Mr. Perfect, Miss Right

Overview: Kids will create the "perfect" man and woman for a blind date.

Game Type: Discussion-starter, funny, senior high, suitable for disabled

Group Size: 10 to 20

Time Involved: 30 to 45 minutes

Supplies: Paper; pencils; and an assortment of men's and women's clothing, makeup, wigs, shoes, and accessories

Preparation: None

Have all the girls form one group and all the guys form another group. Explain that in this game, the girls will create the "perfect" man for a blind date, and the guys will create the "perfect" woman for a blind date—both complete with perfect clothing, demeanor, and speech.

Distribute paper and pencils, and give the kids two to three minutes to write down what they would want in a perfect man or woman. Girls should write their consensus of what they desire in a perfect man, and guys should write their consensus of what they want in a perfect woman. When groups have finished, collect the papers, and keep them until the game is over—without letting either team see what the other team wrote.

Next, invite the guys and girls to go into different dressing rooms and create the perfect man and woman for a mystery date. You can have the girls produce what they consider a perfect woman and the guys produce what they consider a perfect man, or you can have the girls produce the perfect man and the guys produce the perfect woman. Allow fifteen minutes for this make-over.

After both groups have completed their make-overs, bring out the mystery couple, and allow each team to see what the other has produced. Allow the man and woman to talk to each other or "strut their stuff" if they like. Then read the descriptions of the perfect man and woman the teams wrote earlier. See how these ideals were similar to or different from what each group actually delivered.

Use this game to lead into a discussion on expectations we place on the opposite sex, dating, relationships, or sexuality.

MY FAVORITE HOBBY

Overview: Kids will try to decide what hobbies group members are involved in.

Game Type: No supplies and no preparation, quiet, suitable for disabled

Group Size: 2 to 10

Time Involved: 10 to 20 minutes

Supplies: None

Preparation: None

Ask kids each to think of two hobbies they enjoy—anything they enjoy doing during their free time. Then ask kids each to add a third hobby to their lists; this hobby should be something they don't actually do but would like to do someday. For example, Ray's list of three hobbies may include photography and biking—activities he currently enjoys—and also rock-climbing—an activity he hasn't done but would like to.

After kids have thought of their hobbies, have each person state his or her list. After each list, have the group vote on which one of the three is the future hobby. See how well your kids know how others spend their free time.

NAME THAT RADIO TUNE

Overview: Kids will guess the titles to songs being played on the radio.

Game Type: Discussion-starter, musical, suitable for disabled

Group Size: 20 to 30

Time Involved: 2 to 10 minutes

Supplies: A Bible, a radio, paper, and pen

Preparation: None

Have kids sit in a circle near the radio, and explain that you're going to test their knowledge of the various styles of modern music. Tell them that you'll scan through the radio stations and that they should stand up as soon as they can name the artist and the song being played.

Turn the radio on, and begin moving from one station to the next. When you hit a radio station playing a song, stop and wait a few seconds for someone to stand up. If someone stands up, turn down the volume. Allow the first standing person to name that tune. If the group agrees that he or she is correct in naming both the artist and the song, award the person two points. If the person can guess only one or the other, award one point. If no one else can confirm or deny their accuracy, assume the person is correct. If the person fails to answer either or both questions, allow the second person standing to guess.

After someone has named that tune—or if no one stands up after a few seconds—continue to the next station. Be sure to keep going until you've heard a variety of musical styles.

When you have gone through the range of stations, congratulate the person with the most points. Then ask:

- **Were some musical styles easier for you to guess than others? Why or why not?**
- **Why were some artists easier for you to identify than others?**
- **What did this game teach you about other members of the group?**

Read aloud John 10:14, and say:

Just as each of you has learned to recognize the voice and style of the artist you listen to the most, Jesus wants us to practice listening to and recognizing his voice. He wants us to be ready to respond to him and follow his lead.

Nature Scavenger Hunt

Overview: Kids will get to know each other as they mentally collect items from nature.

Game Type: Active, discussion-starter, outside, suitable for disabled

Group Size: Any

Time Involved: 30 to 45 minutes

Supplies: Paper and pencils

Preparation: None

Have kids form pairs, and give each pair paper and a pencil. Explain that the group will go on a walk or hike together and that each pair is responsible for writing down ten things they see that they're both thankful for. Emphasize that the goal isn't simply to write down ten things; the goal is to discover what each person is thankful for and list the common things.

After the hike, gather kids together to see what they found. Use this game to lead into a discussion about how friendships can be formed through common interests or about how sharing faith is easier when people discover their common concerns.

Newly-Met Game

Overview: Kids will learn about each other and then answer questions for funny results.

Game Type: Funny, icebreaker, suitable for disabled

Group Size: 2 to 10

Time Involved: 20 to 30 minutes

Supplies: Newsprint, tape, index cards, a watch and markers

Preparation: On the newsprint, write, "Grandparents," "Strange Pets," "History," and "Becoming Famous." Then tape the newsprint to a wall. Be sure to ask for an adult volunteer to help you with this game.

Have kids form pairs.

Say: **You're going to play a game to learn more about your partner. You'll each have three minutes to tell your partner about yourself using the categories listed on the newsprint.**

<table>
<tr><td>

LEADER TIP

Of course, you can choose five different subjects and make up your own questions for kids to answer. You may want to tailor the questions more specifically to your group, your town, or even what you're studying.

</td><td>

Let kids know when three minutes have passed so each partner gets three minutes to talk. Then after another three minutes, distribute index cards and markers to everyone. Explain that pairs will separate, answer questions, and then come back together to see how well the pairs know each other.

Have one partner from each pair go to another room with an adult volunteer to answer the questions. Have kids number their index cards from one to four. Then on the back of the corresponding cards, have kids write answers to the following questions:

</td></tr>
</table>

- **What is (was) your maternal grandmother's first name?**
- **If you had a pet elephant, what would you name it?**
- **If you had a time machine, what time period would you most like to travel to?**
- **If you could be famous for something for fifteen minutes, what would it be?**

When kids have finished writing their answers, instruct them to keep the number side of the index cards up and the answer side down until it's time to reveal the answers.

Bring both groups together again. Have one pair sit in front of everyone else. Ask one person in the pair the first question, and have that person say what he or she thinks the partner answered. After the first person offers an answer, have the partner flip over the index card to reveal the true answer. If the first person answered correctly, award the team one thousand points. Repeat the process with all the questions and then with the other person in the pair. Continue until all pairs have had a chance to participate. The pair with the most points wins.

Oingo-Boingo

Overview: Kids will attempt to work together to jump a rope.

Game Type: Active, funny, junior high

Group Size: Any

Time Involved: 2 to 10 minutes

Supplies: Jump-ropes

Preparation: None

Have kids form teams of three, and give each team a jump-rope. The object of the game is for team members to each jump the rope twenty-five times.

Two team members should hold the ends of the rope while the third team member jumps the rope twenty-five times. For each jump, team members must shout together, "[Number] oingo-boingo!" When one team member has finished jumping, the second and then the third must jump. If someone misses a jump, he or she must start over with "One oingo-boingo!" The first team to finish wins.

> **VARIATION**
>
> Establish a starting line and a finish line, and have teams jump rope and move across the playing area at the same time.

Phone Tag

Overview: Kids will phone others in the group to pass on who's "It."

Game Type: Quiet, suitable for disabled

Group Size: Any

Time Involved: More than 1 hour

Supplies: A list of your group members' phone numbers

Preparation: Photocopy the list of phone numbers.

Call a student, and explain that he or she is "It" in a game of phone tag and must call someone else in the group and pass "It" on. Have kids pass on these rules:

- You must actually speak to the person—no answering machines or messages left with little sisters.

- If someone has already been "It," you have to call someone else until you find someone who hasn't been "It" yet. For example, you begin by calling Melanie, who calls Michael, who calls Teresa. If Teresa calls Melanie, she will have to call someone else instead.

- Everyone must have been "It" by the next meeting.

At first, the game shouldn't present much of a challenge except in trying to reach a real person. But after the game has been going for a while, "It" may have to make several phone calls to find someone who hasn't been "It" yet. At the next meeting, find out who was last "It" and how long the game lasted.

> ## VARIATION
>
> To encourage further friend-making, ask "It" to talk for at least thirty seconds with the people he or she calls before asking if they've been "It" yet. You could also give kids a question to discuss and pass on—for example, "If your life was a color, what color would it be and why?"

PICNIC ANYONE?

Overview: Kids will try to figure out what they can take to join the leader on a "picnic."

Game Type: Junior high, no supplies and no preparation, quiet, suitable for disabled, travel

Group Size: 20 to 30

Time Involved: 2 to 10 minutes

Supplies: None

Preparation: None

Have kids sit in a circle. Explain that you're going on a picnic and that anyone who wants to can join you as long as he or she brings an appropriate item. The key is that the picnic item must start with the same letters as the person's first and last name. For example, if your name is Ryan Nielsen, you'd start the game by saying:

I am Ryan Nielsen, and I'm bringing red napkins.

After you state what you're bringing, turn to the next person and ask what he or she bringing. If kids follow the correct pattern, say:

Great. Please join me on my picnic.

If kids don't follow the correct pattern, say:

I'm sorry, but you can't come on my picnic,

and then move on to the next person. Continue asking people until everyone has figured out the pattern.

Pillow Pass-Over

Overview: Kids will pull opponents toward a pillow and try to avoid the pillow themselves.

Game Type: Active

Group Size: 10 to 20

Time Involved: 2 to 10 minutes

Supplies: A sofa pillow

Preparation: Clear the playing area of furniture and other obstacles.

Have kids form two equal teams. Then have teams form a large circle, with one team forming half of the circle and the other team forming the other half. Have everyone hold hands, and place the sofa pillow in the center of the circle.

At your signal, each side should begin pulling, trying to make some player from the other team touch the sofa pillow. Players may jump to avoid the pillow, but they must keep holding hands. As soon as a player touches the pillow, he or she must drop out of the circle. If players let go of each other's hands, both players are out.

After about five minutes of strenuous pulling and jumping, the team with more players left in the game wins.

Pillow Talk

Overview: Kids will take turns sitting on a pillow while answering questions.

Game Type: Mixer, quiet, suitable for disabled

Group Size: 10 to 20

Time Involved: 10 to 20 minutes

Supplies: A pillow or beanbag that's large enough for at least three teenagers to sit on

Preparation: None

Have kids form a circle around the pillow. Invite three teenagers to sit on the pillow. Tell the three kids that you'll ask them some questions and that they should shout out their responses. If two or more of these kids shout out the same answer, they may continue to sit on the pillow. If any or all, however, have different responses, they must leave the pillow and allow new kids from the circle to take their place.

This is an easy game that will reveal a great many "facts" about people in a short amount of time. Allow everyone to have a chance to sit on the pillow, and see who can remain on the pillow for the longest period of time.

Use these questions or create others to fit your group:

- What soap did you use to bathe today?
- What brand of toothpaste do you use?
- What color are the walls in your bedroom?
- What's under your bed right now?
- What's your favorite color?
- What's your favorite subject in school?
- What do you normally carry in the back pocket of your jeans?
- How many watts is the light bulb in your bedroom?
- What's under the front seat of your car (or a parent's car)?
- What did you eat for dinner yesterday?

PIZZA-SHAPE CONTEST

Overview: Kids will nibble pieces of pizza into recognizable shapes.

Game Type: Food, icebreaker, suitable for disabled

Group Size: 2 to 10

Time Involved: 10 to 20 minutes

Supplies: Pizza, napkins, drinks, and small prizes for contest winners

Preparation: None

Need an icebreaker at a pizza party? Kids will enjoy this opportunity to play with their food and compete for prizes.

Pass out one slice of pizza to each player, and have kids try to nibble their pizza slices into recognizable shapes. Allow ten minutes for nibbling; then have kids display their shapes. Have kids vote for the most recognizable shape, most unusual shape, smallest recognizable shape, and any other category you can think of. The more "winners," the better!

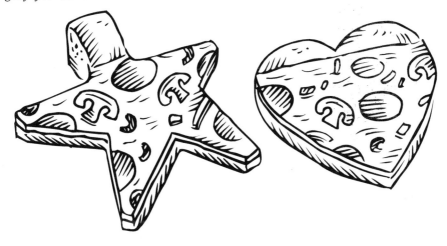

Play That Tune

Overview: Kids will form their own musical groups to express their personal tastes and interests.

Game Type: Funny, musical, suitable for disabled

Group Size: Any

Time Involved: 45 to 60 minutes

Supplies: Newsprint; markers; small hand "instruments," including kitchen pots, pans, and spoons; and assorted props such as hats, clothes, and jewelry

Preparation: None

Have kids form groups of four to six. Kids will design their own musical group by deciding what type of music they'll play, who will play the group's different roles, what their group will be known for, and what their stage show will be. Tell the kids to select a group name and a key verse or slogan. Let

the groups use the supplies to create their own sound and style. Suggest
themes, such as Hawaiian, country, jazz, rhythm and blues, hip-hop, classical, pop, alternative, and rock.

LEADER TIP

You may want to take photographs of the musical groups and even record their performances on a cassette tape or videotape.

Give kids about twenty minutes to create a performance that includes a band introduction and a musical sample.

When groups have finished, have each group perform for everyone. Lead kids in applauding each performance. Although the game's fun is in creating a band, you may want to have kids vote for "Most Promising Band."

POWER PILLOW

Overview: Kids will play a pillow version of Musical Chairs.

Game Type: Icebreaker, mixer, suitable for disabled

Group Size: 20 to 30

Time Involved: 10 to 20 minutes

Supplies: A cassette player or a CD player, a cassette tape or a CD, and sitting pillows that are large enough for two people to sit on. Bring enough pillows to accommodate your entire group.

Preparation: None

Invite kids to sit on a pillow next to someone they don't know very well. Then ask a question to generate some conversation. (See the sample questions below.)

After about a minute, turn on the music, and have kids walk around. Remove a pillow, and then turn off the music. When the music stops, each person must find a new partner and a pillow to sit on. If kids don't find a pillow, they must sit out. Have partners discuss another question, and have kids that are sitting out discuss the question, too. Then continue the game until only one pair remains.

Here are some possible questions and topics:

- **Tell about a time when you were scared silly.**
- **Describe the best amusement park ride you've ever ridden.**

- Describe what your toes look like.
- What's your best talent?
- Describe the most beautiful place you've seen.
- What's one of your life goals?
- Who's your favorite recording artist?
- What's your favorite TV show?
- What are your vacation plans?
- Describe your bedroom.
- What kind of job would you like someday?
- If you could live anywhere, where would you live?
- Describe a perfect meal.
- What's your favorite Bible verse?
- Describe your favorite T-shirt.

RANSOM-NOTE AFFIRMATIONS

Overview: Kids will create affirmation "ransom notes."

Game Type: Affirmation, funny, quiet, suitable for disabled

Group Size: Any

Time Involved: 30 to 45 minutes

Supplies: Paper, pens, a hat, magazines, newspapers, scissors, glue sticks, and tacks or tape

Preparation: Write each group member's name on a piece of paper, and put the papers in a hat.

Set out the supplies. Ask kids to each draw a name (not their own) and not share the name with anyone.

Say: **Look through the magazines and newspapers, and cut out letters or words to form a "ransom note" for the person whose name you drew. This note should summarize what you think your friend is worth, and why. Glue your ransom note together on a sheet of paper, but don't reveal your identity. Be sure to mention your friend's name in the note, however.**

Allow kids to spread out to complete this task. A sample ransom note might read, "Friends and family of John Doe, please leave one trillion dollars in unmarked bills in the parking lot of Good Samaritan Church. Johnny is worth every bit of a trillion because he's a great friend. He's always willing to help someone who's hurting, and he makes good grades, too! Better bring the money, or we'll dump pickle juice on his head like we did at the retreat last summer. An anonymous friend."

After kids have completed their ransom notes, collect the notes, and hang them on a wall. These notes will be a source of inspiration and fun for weeks to come, and kids will have a great time trying to guess who wrote them.

ROPE RELAY

Overview: Kids will create shapes with rope to represent themselves.

Game Type: Suitable for disabled, team-building

Group Size: Any

Time Involved: 10 to 20 minutes

Supplies: Two ropes of the same length. Each group member will need about two feet of rope.

Preparation: None

Have kids form two equal teams. Give each team a rope.

Say: **Each member of your team must choose a shape or form that represents something important about himself or herself. The whole team must then work together to create that shape with the rope. Everyone has to be touching the rope, and the form representing each person must be something unique. You can't create the same form twice. As soon as you've finished the first shape, move immediately to the next. Your team is finished when you've created a form for each person on the team.**

Start the game. The team that finishes first wins.

SACK RELAY

Overview: Kids will complete a relay in which they affirm other group members.

Game Type: Affirmation, funny, mixer, suitable for disabled

Group Size: 20 to 30

Time Involved: 2 to 10 minutes

Supplies: Large sacks, scissors, and the "Relay Instructions" handout (p. 186)

Preparation: Make photocopies of the "Relay Instructions" handout (p. 186), and cut apart the instructions. Place one set of instructions into a sack for each team of four.

Have kids form teams of four, and have teams stand behind a designated starting line. Across the room from each team, place a chair and a sack with slips of paper in it.

Say: **When I say "go," a member from your team will run across the room to the chair facing you, grab a slip of paper from the sack, read it, and then follow the directions precisely. After you read a slip, do not put it back into the sack. When you complete the task, tag the next person on your team. The team that gets through all the slips in its sack first is the winner. Remember, you must do exactly what it says on the paper. Also, when someone asks for your team's cooperation, you must help them.**

Start the relay, and watch for lots laughter and fun.

Relay Instructions

1. Go to someone on another team, and whisper, "I'm glad you're in our group."

 2. Go to someone on another team, and give him or her a back rub for thirty seconds. You must count the seconds out loud.

3. Go to another team, give them high fives, and tell them, "You're cool!"

 4. Go to someone on another team, and trade shoes with him or her until the game's over.

5. Go back to your team, and gather everyone around you. Tell them all to hug you at the same time.

6. Go to someone of the opposite sex on another team, kneel down in front of that person, and ask, "Will you marry me?" Keep asking until he or she says "yes."

7. Go back to your own team. Have two or three team members carry you to the chair and back.

SHAKE AND STOMP

Overview: Kids will greet each other with shakes and stomps.

Game Type: Mixer, suitable for disabled

Group Size: Any

Time Involved: 10 to 20 minutes

Supplies: A pen and slips of paper

Preparation: On each slip of paper, write two numbers with a slash between them—1/3 and 2/4, for example. Prepare one slip for each group member, and use each number combination twice. For example, you could write "1/3" on two slips, "2/4" on two slips, and so on until you have a slip for each group member.

The numbers represent a number of handshakes and then a number of foot stomps. You'll have to calculate what number combinations to use so only two group members have the same number combination. The wider the range of the number of handshakes, the funnier the players' reactions. The closer together the number of foot stomps, the more excitement in the game. For example, if ten kids are in your group, prepare these slips: two slips with 1/3; two slips with 1/4; two slips with 3/1; two slips with 3/2; and two slips with 5/1.

Distribute the slips of paper, and tell kids to keep what their slips say a secret. Explain that the first number is the number of handshakes kids will use and the second number is the number of foot stomps kids will use. Tell kids they'll need to find the person in the group with the same number of handshakes and foot stomps.

This is how the game works: Kids begin by saying their names and shaking each other's hands the number of times indicated on their slips of paper. If their number of handshakes isn't the same, they move to someone new.

When they meet someone with the same number of handshakes, they stomp their feet the number of times indicated on their slips of paper. If their foot stomps are not the same, they move to someone new.

When kids find their partners—the person with the same number of handshakes and foot stomps—they step aside and watch the other kids complete their searches.

To make sure no one's made a mistake, everyone—even the last two kids—should complete the process of saying their names and then matching their handshakes and foot stomps. When everyone is finished, have kids applaud each other.

THE SHAPE OF US

Overview: Kids will create "sculptures" to represent themselves.

Game Type: Quiet, suitable for disabled

Group Size: 10 to 20

Time Involved: 10 to 20 minutes

Supplies: Scissors, tape, string, straws, and pipe cleaners

Preparation: None

Have kids form trios. Set out the supplies, and then tell trios to create a three-dimensional sculpture to represent who they are as a group. First, each group member should use the supplies to create a representation of who he or she is. Then group members should put their representations together to create a group sculpture.

When groups have finished, have them explain their sculptures to everyone.

SLIDERS

Overview: Kids will slide around on an upside-down table.

Game Type: Active, discussion-starter, team-builder

Group Size: 10 to 20

Time Involved: 2 to 10 minutes

Supplies: A watch and a large table you can turn upside down or a large, flattened cardboard box

Preparation: Find a carpeted area in which kids can slide around on an upside-down table or flattened box. Clear away any obstacles.

Ask a volunteer to stand on the table or box. Have the rest of the group spread around. Explain that a "rescue boat captain"—the volunteer—is busy trying to rescue "survivors"—all other group members—from a shipwreck.

In order to board, a survivor must give his or her full name and provide one reason to live. Encourage players to think seriously about their responses. Then a survivor grabs the captain's hand and boards the "boat." Both players continue by sliding the table across the floor. Note that to move the table, players will have to keep one foot inside and one outside, sliding it across the floor. Inform the group that the captain has only one minute to get as many people on board as possible. Lengthen or shorten the time of play depending on the group size.

When time is up, have kids gather around the table. Ask:

- What was the most challenging thing about the activity?
- What was it like to wait to board the ship?
- What was it like to help guide the ship in picking up survivors?
- To those who did not get on board, what was it like to be left out?

Read aloud John 15:13, and then ask:

- What can this game teach us about the value of friendship?

SNOWY CONNECT-THE-DOTS

Overview: Kids will draw pictures in the snow.

Game Type: Active, outside, winter

Group Size: Any

Time Involved: 10 to 20 minutes

Supplies: Snow and bottles of dye or colored liquids

Preparation: None

Have kids form trios, and give each trio a bottle of dye. Explain that trios are going to create connect-the-dots patterns for another trio to draw a picture from—but they're going to do this in the snow.

Take kids outside, and have trios spread out so they have at least five square feet of space. Have trios think about a picture they'd like to create and then squirt dye dots in the snow to create the connect-the-dots pattern.

When trios have finished, have them rotate to different pictures. Have the trio members work together to stomp in the snow to connect the dots together. When they've connected the dots, have them call out what the picture is.

Before going back inside, have everyone walk around to admire all the artistry.

SQUIGGLERS

Overview: Kids will pass a ball between the feet of a group standing in a circle.

Game Type: Active, discussion-starter, outside, team-builder

Group Size: Any

Time Involved: 2 to 10 minutes

Supplies: A soccer ball

Preparation: None

Have kids stand in a boy-girl-boy-girl circle. If there aren't an even number of guys and girls, disperse the "extras" throughout the circle. Ask players to lock arms with each other.

Place a ball on floor between the feet of any player. Explain that players are to pass the ball to the *right* using only their feet. Add that the ball must be passed in an in-and-out pattern. (See diagram.) As players pass the ball, they must say their names. The next person must say, "Thank you, [previous player's name]. My name is [his or her name]."

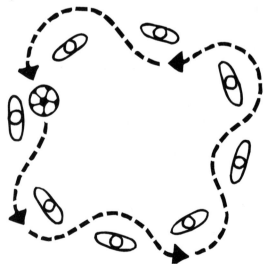

Start the game, and see how long it takes to pass the ball around the circle. Then have kids repeat the game by passing the ball in the other direction. After the ball has completed the circle, see who can name everyone in the group.

This game can help bring groups closer, and you can use it as a discussion-starter for studies on building friendships and strengthening group unity.

> ## VARIATION
>
> Have kids pass two balls in different directions—at the same time! You can also vary the information kids provide—middle name, favorite dessert, or favorite sport or hobby, for example.

STUCK ON YOU

Overview: Kids will stick happy face affirmation notes on each other.

Game Type: Affirmation, discussion-starter, mixer, suitable for disabled, team-builder

Group Size: Any

Time Involved: 2 to 10 minutes

Supplies: Sticky notes and markers

Preparation: None

Give each person ten to twenty sticky notes and a marker. Tell kids to draw a happy face on each note and put their initials under it.

Say: **When I say "go," I want you to walk to other people as fast as you can and stick one of your happy face notes on them. When you do, give that person a compliment. For example, you might say, "You have a great smile" or "You are one of the kindest people I know." You must give the person a compliment before sticking a note on him or her. The object of the game is to be the first person to get one of your notes on every one else in the group.**

Say "go," and watch the fun begin. When everyone has placed a sticky note on everyone else, have kids discuss these questions:

- **What was it like to receive compliments and happy faces?**
- **In what ways do you think giving people compliments builds friendships in our group?**

- How is a compliment like leaving someone with a happy face sticker?

TEAM KEEP-AWAY

Overview: Kids will play a version of keep-away that emphasizes teamwork.

Game Type: Active, discussion-starter, outside, team-builder

Group Size: 10 to 20

Time Involved: 10 to 20 minutes

Supplies: A ball

Preparation: None

Have kids form two teams. Explain that teammates will try to throw a ball back and forth to one another while the other team tries to intercept the throw. A team scores one point every time members complete three consecutive passes—to three different teammates—without an interception. The first team to score five points wins.

After a team scores five points, lead into a discussion about the game. For example, kids could discuss how they had to learn others' skills and find ways to help each other succeed. Have kids compare what it took to succeed in the game to what it takes to succeed in any group.

THREE-WAY CONVERSATIONS

Overview: Kids will participate in a unique three-way conversation and then introduce one another to the group.

Game Type: Funny, icebreaker, suitable for disabled

Group Size: Any

Time Involved: 20 to 30 minutes

Supplies: A watch

Preparation: None

Have kids form groups of three. Instruct the students that they are going to have three minutes each to tell who they are and something about themselves. Give them some suggestions, such as name, age, school, favorite color, favorite subject, and so on. In addition, instruct kids that they're going to have to talk for the entire three minutes—they can't stop early. Also tell kids that after they talk, each person will have to stand up and introduce another member of the small group to the entire group, so they need to pay very close attention.

Here's the catch that makes the game more fun and interesting. Instruct the teams that they're going to sit down with one person in the middle and with the other two sitting on either side of and facing the middle person. The two outside people will talk at the same time. The person in the middle will have to try to listen to both people.

Start the game, and call "time" after three minutes. Then have group members rotate so a new person is sitting in the middle. After another three minutes, have group members rotate one last time.

Afterward, have each person stand up and introduce another group member. Be sure to ask everyone to introduce a different person.

Tick-Tack Relays

Overview: Kids will collect breath mints and play games with the mints.

Game Type: Discussion-starter, funny, suitable for disabled

Group Size: Any

Time Involved: 20 to 30 minutes

Supplies: Well-sharpened pencils, breath mints, paper, a pen, and other supplies as you choose. (See below.)

Preparation: None

Give each student a breath mint for every person in the group and a pencil. Have kids write their initials with pencil on every mint. Then direct kids to trade one mint with every group member.

Then have kids use the breath mints to play games, such as a mint javelin throw, mint high jump, mints-on-a-spoon relay, one-mint-on-a-knife relay, push-the-mint-with-your-nose race, and so on. Warn kids to keep track of all their original mints during the games.

As kids play the games, subtly jot down what students say as they treasure or trash the mints. For example, you could write down comments such as these: "Oh well, I lost one. No big deal" or "Oh, that's my Megan mint. I can't lose that one!"

After the games, gather kids together. Explain that trading the mints was an analogy to friendship and that we can choose to treasure or trash our friends. Read aloud some of the statements you jotted down, but leave out identifying details or condemnation. For example, translate "Oh, that's my Megan mint. I can't lose that one!" to "Oh, that's my name-of-someone mint. I can't lose that one!" Ask:

- **How is what we did with our mints similar to and different from the way we treat each other in this group?**
- **How did we favor some mints more than others? (Don't name the mints—just give examples.) Why?**
- **What changes might God recommend in you to give you good friendship "breath"?**

TIRE ALIGNMENT

Overview: Kids will balance on tires as they get to know each other.

Game Type: Active, icebreaker, outside

Group Size: 20 to 30

Time Involved: 2 to 10 minutes

Supplies: A fourteen-inch tire for every ten players. Ask service stations, tire centers, or church members if you can borrow old or spare tires.

Preparation: Place the tires outside and apart from each other.

Have kids form teams of eight to ten, and have each team stand at a tire.

Say: **Every team member must get onto the tire. When everyone's on the tire, every person must take a turn telling his or her favorite book title. If anyone touches the ground, everyone must get off the tire to begin again.**

This may initially seem like an easy task, but teams will soon learn that they need to plan carefully and help team members stay balanced. Have teams balance several times with additional questions or topics. Here are some ideas:

- **What country would you most like to visit?**
- **How many uncles do you have?**
- **What's the most recent movie you've seen?**
- **Who's your all-time favorite teacher?**
- **What was the name of your first pet?**

TIRE BOWLING

Overview: Kids will go "bowling"—for free!

Game Type: Active, outside

Group Size: 10 to 20

Time Involved: 10 to 20 minutes

Supplies: An old car tire without the rim or inner tube, sand, ten empty two-liter soda bottles, paper, and pens

Preparation: Fill each soda bottle with enough sand so it won't easily blow down.

Have kids form two teams. Set up the soda bottles as bowling pins at one end of your playing area. Designate a starting line your bowlers can't cross.

Players of one team will take turns rolling the tire toward the bottles, and the other teams will reset the "pins." Unlike real bowling, each player will get only one shot per frame. Let each team member bowl for ten frames.

If a player scores a strike, knocking all the pins down, count his or her next frame double. If a player scores a strike on the tenth frame, give the bowler an extra shot. Keep score for each team.

You'll want to keep these bowling supplies in a storage area to use again and again.

TOGETHER PICTURES

Overview: Kids will compose pictures one line at a time.

Game Type: Affirmation, discussion-starter, quiet, suitable for disabled, team-builder

Group Size: 2 to 10

Time Involved: 10 to 20 minutes

Supplies: Paper and colorful markers

Preparation: None

Have kids sit in a circle, and place the markers in the center of the circle. Distribute paper, and have kids write their initials on the backs of their papers. Then direct kids each to make one mark on the paper that signifies something good about the group. Next, have kids pass their papers to the right so the next person can add a mark. Continue until kids' original papers come back to them.

As kids draw, encourage them to make each picture different, depending on what each picture looks like when they get it. Emphasize that each picture should be meaningful instead of a collection of stray marks.

When kids have finished drawing, ask:

- **What are your impressions of the group picture that got back to you?**
- **What marks do you make on other group members' lives?**
- **How do your marks combine with others' marks to make the picture better?**
- **What kinds of marks do you sometimes make that mess up the picture?**
- **What marks will you choose to make as a result of this game?**

TRIVIA RETREAT

Overview: Kids will play a unique trivia game to learn more about group members.

Game Type: Funny, suitable for disabled, travel

Group Size: 20 to 30

Time Involved: 20 to 30 minutes

Supplies: Paper and pens

Preparation: None

Have kids form two teams, and give each team paper and pens. Ask each team to come up with ten to fifteen zany trivia questions to ask the other team. These should be strange-but-true facts about teenagers in the group—for example, "Can you name the person who has a dog named Dingo?" "Which member of our group once ate an entire cheeseburger in one bite?" "Which group member owns a rare 1934 silver dollar?"

When kids have written their questions, have them ask each other the questions. Award one point for each correct answer.

TV Ties

Overview: Kids will form groups by TV characters.

Game Type: Mixer, suitable for disabled

Group Size: 20 to 30

Time Involved: 2 to 10 minutes

Supplies: Name tags and a marker

Preparation: Write the first names of the following TV characters on individual name tags:
- *I Love Lucy*–Lucy, Ricky, Fred, and Ethel
- *Gilligan's Island*–Gilligan, Skipper, the Professor, Mary Ann, Ginger, Mr. Howell, Mrs. Howell
- *The Addams Family*–Gomez, Morticia, Uncle Fester, Grandmama, Pugsley, Wednesday, Lurch, Cousin Itt
- *The Brady Bunch*–Mike, Carol, Greg, Peter, Bobby, Marcia, Cindy, Jan

Give each teenager a name tag. Then have kids walk around the room and try to find all of their other cast members. When all the cast members have found each other, they must sing the theme song from their TV show to win.

Video Conference Call

Overview: Kids will replicate a pose and pass it along.

Game Type: Funny, no supplies and no preparation, quiet

Group Size: Any

Time Involved: 2 to 10 minutes

Supplies: None

Preparation: None

Tell kids they're going to play a game based on new technology—the video conference call. Have kids stand in a single-file line; designate half of the line as one team and the other half as another team. Have the two teams face away from each other. Stand in the middle of the line, between the two teams.

Explain that you'll strike a pose for the first two players, who will turn to face you. Those players must turn to the next players on their teams, replicate your pose exactly, and then touch the next player's shoulder so he or she can replicate the pose. When the last two members of each team receive the pose, they should walk in front of the teams, face each other, and strike the pose to see which team's video conference call went through.

Choose a pose that includes a facial expression. Touch the first two players simultaneously, and display the pose. After the teams have passed the pose, have the two players who were at the end of the lines move to the front of the lines to receive a new video conference call.

WE'VE GOT RHYTHM

Overview: Kids will compare individual rhythms to group rhythms.

Game Type: Discussion-starter, musical, suitable for disabled, team-builder

Group Size: 20 to 30

Time Involved: 20 to 30 minutes

Supplies: Rhythm instruments of all kinds—maracas, bongos, congas, tambourines, sticks, and anything else that makes a sound

Preparation: None

Distribute the instruments. Start by having kids make whatever noises they want on their instruments.

After about three minutes of noise, have kids form four groups by instrument type, if possible. Instruct the first group to play a "1, 2, 3, 4" beat and keep playing. Instruct the second group to play a "one-and-two, three-and-four" beat in time with the first group. Instruct the third group to play a triplet on the first and third beats—a "one-and-and, pause, three-and-and, pause" beat. Instruct fourth group to play two beats for every one count—a "one-and-two-and-three-and four-and" beat. Have groups play their respective rhythms alone and then together.

Discuss the difference in overall sound between the first and the second experience. Encourage kids to share their opinions. Some people will experience a more cooperative mood with the unstructured sound, and some will experience a more cooperative mood with the more structured sound.

WHERE'S THE FOOD?

Overview: Kids will find clues to help them through a progressive dinner.

Game Type: Discussion-starter, food, night, suitable for disabled

Group Size: 10 to 20

Time Involved: More than 1 hour

Supplies: A salad, a main course, a dessert, supplies for kids to eat and clean up the meal, index cards, and a pen

Preparation: Secretly arrange for three houses to host the kids for these dinner courses: salad, main course, dessert. Then recruit volunteers to hold clues around the town so cars filled with group members can find them and proceed to each house. Place the clues so kids will have to drive only a few blocks from the clues to the houses. Recruit additional volunteers to ride with or drive the kids and provide help if kids

get lost or can't figure out the clues. Be sure
volunteer drivers understand that they're to drive
only where kids tell them to drive.

Write clues on index cards, and hide the clues
around your town. Clues should begin at your
meeting area and should take kids to at least one
place between each house.

Have kids form groups based on how many kids can ride in cars, and be
sure to provide a volunteer for each vehicle. Give each group the first clue,
and let them know that if they can't find the first location within ten
minutes, they should get the information from the volunteer.

When kids get to the clue sites, the volunteers there should show the kids
the next clue. Be sure these volunteers know how many cars to expect so
they don't have to wait longer than necessary.

When all the kids have arrived at the meal site and have eaten that por-
tion of the meal, hand out the next clue and send them on their way.

After the dessert at the last house, ask:

- **What did you like most about this experience?**
- **What are some new things you learned about the people in your car?**
- **What was the funniest thing that happened during this experience?**
- **Why do you think it's important for us to spend time getting to know each other better?**

WHO'S THAT?

Overview: Kids will gather strange and unusual facts group
members.

Game Type: Icebreaker, quiet, suitable for disabled, travel

Group Size: 20 to 30

Time Involved: 20 to 30 minutes

Supplies: Index cards, pencils, and a watch

Preparation: None

Have kids form pairs, and distribute index cards and pencils.

Say: **I'd like each pair to find a quiet place to talk. You have ten** minutes to interview your partners and find out as many interesting or unique facts about each other as you can. Write these facts on your index cards. For example, if your partner has an unknown talent or award, write that down. Or if your partner has met someone famous, write that down. Use your imagination.

After ten minutes, collect the index cards. Shuffle them, and then read them aloud, one by one, to the entire group. Have kids guess the identity of each person described on the cards.

If your kids need some intriguing questions, suggest some of these:
- What's the wildest thing you've ever done?
- In five words, how would you describe yourself to someone else?
- What is your pet peeve?
- Do you have any bad habits?
- What's the best thing you've ever done for someone else?

Worm Wrestling

Overview: Kids will play a fun wrestling game that's perfect for a retreat or lock-in.

Game Type: Active, funny

Group Size: Any

Time Involved: 10 to 20 minutes

Supplies: Masking tape and two sleeping bags with drawstring necks

Preparation: None

Have kids form two teams. Use tape to mark a circle about ten feet in diameter in the middle of your playing area, and clear the circle of any obstacles.

Have the first player from each team step into a sleeping bag and pull the drawstring of each bag securely above his or her shoulders. Explain that the object of the game is for one player to cause the other player to cross the line out of the circle. Players can push, pull, or wrestle, but they must stay inside their sleeping bags.

If any part of a player's body or sleeping bag crosses the line, the player is out, and two new opponents begin play. Let everyone have a chance to worm-wrestle.

You're a What?

Overview: Kids will learn each other's names and test their memories.

Game Type: Junior high, no supplies and no preparation, quiet, suitable for disabled, travel

Group Size: Any

Time Involved: 2 to 10 minutes

Supplies: None

Preparation: None

LEADER TIP

If you have a larger group, have kids form circles of twelve.

Have kids form a circle. Have one person say his or her first name and the name of an animal that begins with the same letter as the name. Then have the next person repeat the first person's name and animal before stating his or her own name and animal. Continue until kids have gone all the way around the circle.

HOLIDAY GAMES

New Year's Day

Decade Game

Overview: Kids will work with senior citizens to figure out when events occurred.

Game Type: Discussion-starter, knowledge-builder, service, suitable for disabled

Group Size: 30 to 50

Time Involved: 45 to 60 minutes

Supplies: Poster board, scissors, and a marker

Preparation: Contact a nursing home, and tell them you'd like to bring a group of kids to play a trivia game with the senior citizens on New Year's Day. You can also use this game during an intergenerational church party on New Year's Day.

Cut the poster board into 8x10-inch pieces. For each team of six people, create a set of ten poster board cards with decades written on them: 1900-1909, 1910-1919, 1920s, 1930s, 1940s, 1950s, 1960s, 1970s, 1980s, 1990s. You'll also need to develop a list of events, or you can use the list that we've provided.

Have people form teams with three teenagers and three seniors on each team. Explain that you'll read an event and then team members must confer with each other and hold up the card corresponding to the decade in which the event occurred. Once a team holds up a card, it may not change its answer. Each team is awarded two points for each correct answer, so more than one team may receive points for each event. The first team to receive fifty points wins. Make sure you mix up the events so decades aren't grouped together.

This game will help the kids appreciate New Year's Day as a time to reminisce. After the game, have team members tell one another about a favorite time in their lives.

Here is a list of events you can use for the game:

1900-1909
The Wright brothers first successfully flew an airplane.
The U.S. began building Panama Canal.
The first World Series was played.

1910-1919
Countries fought against each other in World War I.
The *Titanic* sank.
The National Park Service was created.

1920s
Babe Ruth hit sixty home runs for a season record.
The stock market crashed, leading the U.S. into economic depression.
Charles Lindbergh flew the first trans-Atlantic flight.

1930s
The Great Depression devastated the U.S.
Prohibition ended.
The airship *Hindenburg* burned.

1940s
Many countries fought against each other in World War II.
The atomic bomb was first used.
The Cold War began.

1950s
Alaska and Hawaii became states.
The U.S. fought in the Korean War.
The *Sputnik* satellite and the *Explorer* satellite first went into orbit.

1960s
Astronauts first walked on the moon.
Doctors performed the first human heart transplant.
Martin Luther King Jr. spoke at the March on Washington D.C.

1970s
The Vietnam War ended.
President Nixon resigned because of the Watergate scandal.
Some fifty U.S. citizens were taken hostage by Muslim militants.

1980s
Sally Ride became the first U.S. woman in space.
The Berlin wall came down.
The stock market suffered Black Monday.

1990s
The U.S. fought Iraq in the Persian Gulf War.
Timothy McVeigh bombed the Oklahoma City federal building.
Mark McGwire hit seventy home runs for a season record.

EVERYBODY'S FIRST

Overview: Kids will try to be first in line—but "first" will keep changing.

Game Type: Active, discussion-starter, no supplies and no preparation

Group Size: 2 to 10

Time Involved: 2 to 10 minutes

Supplies: None

Preparation: None

Have kids line up single file. Explain that kids are going to celebrate the first day of the new year by playing a game in which everyone tries to be first. Tell kids that you'll call out a number and that position in line becomes the first position. Since everyone wants to be first, kids should scramble to try to put themselves in that position. For example, if you call out the number four, kids will scramble to try to occupy the fourth place in line. Most likely, the line will become a mess. After ten seconds, call out a new number, and watch kids scramble again to be "first." Call out five or six numbers, and then end the game.

Afterward, lead kids into a discussion about how our quest to be first can make things very messy.

MESS-O-MANIA

Overview: Kids will forms groups based on a traditional Southern New Year's Day menu.

Game Type: Mixer, suitable for disabled

Group Size: Any

Time Involved: 2 to 10 minutes

Supplies: Slips of paper, a pen, and a bag

Preparation: On each slip of paper, write one of the following dishes: black-eyed peas, collard greens, cornbread,

and onion. You'll need one strip for each group
member. Fold the strips, and place them in a bag.

Have kids gather together in the center of the room. Have each person
draw a folded strip of paper from the bag, but caution kids not to show their
strips of paper to anyone.

Explain that the group is going to form "meal groups" of four based on the
traditional fare served in the South on New Year's Day: black-eyed peas, collard greens, cornbread, and onions.

Players are to move around the room *describing* their menu items. For example, someone might describe a black-eyed pea by saying, "I'm tiny, almost
round, with a little block dot on my middle." Encourage kids to be creative.
Whenever players meet someone who can help complete the meal, the players lock arms with each other and continue together to complete the meal.

When a meal is complete and all the members are connected, the group
should quickly sit on the floor and yell, "Mmm, good!" The first group to do
so wins.

New Year's Taste-Testing Game

Overview: Kids will taste-test food to see if they can spot quality.

Game Type: Discussion-starter, food, suitable for disabled

Group Size: 20 to 30

Time Involved: 20 to 30 minutes

Supplies: A knife, plates, spoons, napkins, paper, a pen, and one
or two snack items in pairs, a "best" and a "regular"
of each food type—for example, homemade cookies
and inexpensive boxed cookies, specialty potato chips
and inexpensive potato chips, and freshly baked bread
and inexpensive plain bread

Preparation: Break or slice the food items into bite-sized pieces,
and place the pieces on plates. Be sure each item
is on its own plate. Then cover the plates with
napkins so kids can't see the differences in the items.

Explain that kids are going to take part in a taste test to see if they can
really taste quality. Have kids line up in front of the covered plates.

Say: **One at a time, approach me and close your eyes. I'll give you a taste of two different items. As you eat each one, decide whether it's the quality item.**

Feed each player one bite of each of the two similar items, making sure to feed the quality item to each person first. When everyone has tasted, ask kids to raise their hands if they think the quality item was the first or second. Everyone who chooses the correct item gets a point.

Have kids line up and try again; repeat the process until kids have tasted all the types of food.

Afterward, lead kids into a discussion about giving God our best during this new year.

TOONIES ON PARADE

Overview: Kids will test their memory of cartoon, TV, and book characters.

Game Type: Quiet, suitable for disabled

Group Size: 2 to 10

Time Involved: 20 to 30 minutes

Supplies: Paper, pens, a VCR, a TV, and a blank videotape

Preparation: Record the Macy's parade for playback during the game.

Have kids gather around the TV, and distribute pens and paper. Explain that the objective of the game is to name as many of the Macy's balloon characters as possible. Without audio, fast-forward through the parade, stopping momentarily on the balloon characters.

After the parade, have kids exchange papers for grading. Rewind the tape, and play it a second time, naming the balloon characters. Who's your group's "toon junkie"?

Martin Luther King Jr.'s Birthday

I Have a Dream

Overview: Kids will affirm their dreams and discover ways God wants them to live out those dreams.

Game Type: Discussion-starter, icebreaker, mixer, quiet, suitable for disabled

Group Size: 20 to 30

Time Involved: 10 to 20 minutes

Supplies: Scissors, paper, and pens

Preparation: Cut out each of the letters "d," "r," "e," "a," and "m" from a half sheet of paper. Cut out enough letters so each person can have at least one.

Give each person a letter, and instruct kids to find people with whom their letters spell the word "dream." If the group does not divide evenly into five, give some kids two letters.

When kids have formed "dream" groups, distribute pens. Then have each person write on one letter a dream he or she has that begins with that letter. For example, for "d," someone might dream for a definite end to violence. If someone has two letters, suggest that the group work together to write a dream for one of the letters.

Have kids tell their group members their dreams, and then have kids trade letters and write new dreams on new letters. Continue until everyone has written five dreams.

Afterward, say:

> Dreams are important. A man named Martin Luther King Jr. dreamed that all people would be judged by their character instead of the color of their skin. His dream was based on the Bible. Ask:
> - How can you tell if a dream you have is based on the Bible?
> - What makes your dreams worth working toward?
> - Where might God want you to begin living out your dream?
> - Dr. King was an eloquent speaker and a dedicated student. With what strengths will God help you achieve your dreams?

- Dr. King promoted nonviolence. What approaches do you think God would want you to use to achieve your dream?
- What would you want to be known for if the nation celebrated your birthday?

After the discussion, assure kids that they can begin achieving their dreams right now.

Up, Up With MLK

Overview: Kids will try to keep Martin Luther King Jr.'s initials from hitting the ground.

Game Type: Active, suitable for disabled

Group Size: Any

Time Involved: 2 to 10 minutes

Supplies: Tissue paper

Preparation: None

Have kids from teams of five, and give each team a few sheets of tissue paper. Have each team tear out Martin Luther King Jr.'s initials from the tissue paper.

Say: **Martin Luther King Jr. inspired—and continues to inspire—people to reach higher. Today you're going to celebrate that in a fun way by trying to keep the initials in the air.**

Explain that teams will lie down so their heads form a tight circle. On your signal, team members will hold up their initials, then let go and try to keep them in the air by blowing.

Say: **Ready? Hold the initials up. Now let go!**

The team that can keep the initials up the longest wins. Play several rounds so kids can formulate a strategy.

Valentine's Day

Achy, Breaky Heart

Overview: Kids will try to secretly pass a heart to each other.

Game Type: Funny, mixer, suitable for disabled

Group Size: 20 to 30

Time Involved: 2 to 10 minutes

Supplies: Pink modeling dough and a small candy prize

Preparation: Form the pink modeling dough into a small heart that kids can easily hide in their hands.

Have kids form a circle. Stand in the center of the circle, and say:

> I'm going to place this heart in someone's hand. You will all walk around and greet each other with handshakes and say, "Happy Valentine's Day." The person with the heart will try to pass it off during handshakes. The person who successfully passes off the heart will count to twenty and then yell, "Oh, my heart! My achy, breaky heart!" without revealing who the heart was passed to.

Have the kids hold out their right hands and close their eyes so you can secretly pass the heart to someone. Shake several kids' hands, too, so kids won't know who got the heart. Then have kids walk around to greet each other.

Have kids play for five to ten minutes. Then award a candy treat to the person left holding the achy, breaky heart.

Connect-a-Heart

Overview: Kids will form phrases with paper hearts taped over their hearts.

Game Type: Mixer, suitable for disabled

Group Size: Any

Time Involved: 2 to 10 minutes

Supplies: Pink or red paper, scissors, a marker, and masking tape

Preparation: Cut hearts out of paper, one heart for each player. Write one word on each heart. Use words that can be linked together to form Valentine's phrases—for example, "Won't you be mine," "You are terrific," and "I think you are great." Use words such as "you," "are," and "love" several times.

Distribute paper hearts, and have kids tape the paper hearts over their chests. Then have the kids walk around. Explain that you're going to call out a phrase, and kids wearing the words of that phrase must find each other and link arms in order.

Call out a common phrase used on Valentine's Day. Start with shorter phrases, and move up to longer phrases. To add to the fun, call out several phrases at the same time.

CUPID'S ARROWS

Overview: Kids will shoot rubber band "arrows."

Game Type: Active, suitable for disabled

Group Size: Any

Time Involved: 2 to 10 minutes

Supplies: Rubber bands, pink or red paper, scissors, tape, and markers

Preparation: From the paper, cut out a heart shape for each group member.

Distribute the hearts and markers, and have each player write on a heart the name of his or her valentine—real or wished-for! Then have kids tape their hearts to a wall.

Have kids line up, shoulder to shoulder, about twenty feet from the wall. Distribute rubber bands, and tell kids they have three chances to hit their valentine with "cupid's arrows." Explain that if they hit a heart—any heart—with a rubber band, they get one point; if they hit their valentine's heart, they get two points.

Say: **On my signal, aim for your valentine. Ready? Aim! Fire!**

After kids shoot their rubber bands, have them each pick up a rubber band from the floor and line up again. Give the signal to shoot again, and have kids retrieve rubber bands and line up again. Give one last signal to shoot. The person with the most points wins. If there's a tie, you can have a shoot-off.

HAVE A HEART

Overview: Kids will see how many red hearts they can collect.

Game Type: Discussion-starter, mixer, suitable for disabled

Group Size: 10 to 20

Time Involved: 2 to 10 minutes

Supplies: Red paper and scissors

Preparation: From the red paper, cut out fifteen one-inch hearts for each person.

Explain that the purpose of this game is for each person to collect as many hearts as possible. Here's how the game works. Give each person fifteen hearts.

Say: **Each of you has fifteen hearts to start the game. You're going to place a number of hearts in your right hand and close your hand over them so no one can see them. You will keep the remaining hearts in** your left hand. Walk up to someone, and ask them to guess how many hearts you're holding in your right hand. If they guess the right number, you have to give them the hearts from your right hand. If they guess the wrong number, they have to give the number of hearts they guessed from their own hearts. We'll see who has the most hearts when time is up. If you run out of hearts, you can ask people who still have hearts to give you some of theirs. Those people may or may not choose to help you out.

Start the game. After a few minutes, call "time," and ask everyone to sit down. Find out who has the most hearts, and declare him or her the "Have-a-Heart" victor. Then ask:

- What was it like when you started losing your hearts?
- What was it like to win a bunch of hearts?
- What was it like when you asked someone to give you some hearts and he or she would or wouldn't?
- What are ways God wants us to share our heart with others?
- What are ways we sometimes refuse to share our hearts with others?

Heart and Sole

Overview: Kids will decorate each other's shoes.

Game Type: Funny, messy, suitable for disabled

Group Size: Any

Time Involved: 10 to 20 minutes

Supplies: Red, pink, purple, and white construction paper; scissors; streamers; bows; wrapped candies; tape; string; and other creative supplies

Preparation: None

Ask students to remove their shoes and place them in a pile while you set out the creative supplies.

Say: **Valentine's Day is often a time for giving gifts. Today you're going to make two valentines—out of your friends' shoes!**

Instruct kids to take two mismatched shoes from the pile and decorate them as best they can with the supplies you've provided.

When kids have finished decorating the shoes, allow kids to search for the shoes' owners and present them with their "sole-ful" valentines. If possible, the owners can then put on the shoes and model their gifts.

Have kids vote either by a show of hands or by secret ballot for the prettiest, cutest, sweetest, and most romantic valentines. Award candy prizes to the winning artists.

LOVE-LETTER SMUGGLING

Overview: Kids will try to move through an obstacle course with "love letters" without getting caught.

Game Type: Bible, discussion-starter

Group Size: 20 to 30

Time Involved: 10 to 20 minutes

Supplies: Bibles, masking tape, blindfolds, and a watch

Preparation: Set up an obstacle course by using masking tape to create "rivers" and furniture to create "mountains" and other barriers.

Tell the kids that since it's Valentine's Day, they're going to smuggle love letters. Explain the obstacle course to the kids, and have them form two groups—the smugglers and the border guards. Have the smugglers line up at the beginning of the obstacle course, and have the guards spread out near the end of the course.

Just before you begin, hand the guards blindfolds. Explain that the smugglers will have to try to move in silence. If a guard hears and points at a smuggler, the smuggler must return to base and start over.

After the guards are blindfolded, hand Bibles to the smugglers. Explain that the Bibles are the love letters they must smuggle across the border. Add that kids will play for five minutes. The smugglers will get a point for each Bible that crosses the border, and the guards will get two points each time they catch a smuggler.

Start the game. After five minutes, call time. Then

LEADER TIP

If you have trouble with guards just pointing randomly all the time, you can penalize them a point for that.

have kids switch roles and play again.

Use this game to lead into a discussion about the "love letter" God gave us, the Bible. Ask:

- **Have you ever read something in the Bible that seemed to be speaking directly to you?**
- **Have you ever experienced troubles or trials and found that something you read in the Bible spoke directly about that?**

Allow time for discussion, and share with kids a Scripture that was God's love letter to you in a time of need.

LOVE-SONG LIP SYNCH

Overview: Kids will experience teamwork while participating in a lip-sync contest.

Game Type: Funny, musical, suitable for disabled

Group Size: Any

Time Involved: 20 to 30 minutes

Supplies: A cassette player or CD player, cassette tapes or CDs of Christian love songs, paper, and markers

Preparation: None

Tell your group that in honor of Valentine's Day, they're going to participate a love-song lip-sync contest. Have pairs volunteer to lip-sync love songs. Have each pair choose a love song, and inform them that they can listen to their song *once*. The object is to be funny, so tell pairs that anything they can do during their song to increase the laughter will help the judges.

While the pairs are listening to the songs they chose, ask for a few volunteers to be the judges. Tell them that their job is to assign a winning title to each pair of contestants—for example, "funniest," "most creative," or "most realistic."

VARIATION

Have the judges sit together. After each duet is finished, have the judges write a number from one to ten on a piece of paper. Have one judge collect the papers and tabulate each pair's final score. When all the contestants have performed, declare a winner.

Another idea is to have every pair lip-sync the same song—either one they're all familiar with or one nobody knows. While pairs are performing, have the rest of the pairs wait in another room so everyone has only one opportunity to listen to the song.

Have each pair perform, and encourage the rest of the group to clap and cheer wildly after each pair has performed. After all the pairs have performed, have the judges confer, write the winning titles on paper, and award each pair a "certificate."

NAME THAT COUPLE

Overview: Kids will attempt to identify their parents by pictures and events.

Game Type: Funny, suitable for disabled

Group Size: 10 to 20

Time Involved: 20 to 30 minutes

Supplies: A slide of each student's parents, index cards, a pen, noisemakers (such as whistles), and a slide projector and screen

Preparation: Contact every student's parents, and ask for a photograph or slide from their early years as a couple. Also ask them to list three notable events in their marriage, preferably something other than kids' births. Have every picture made into a slide at a local photography shop, or copy pictures onto transparency film. Then return the photographs to the parents. Also write each couple's notable events on an index card.

LEADER TIP

If kids live with single parents, use either a picture of the couple or pictures of each parent alone. Be sure to be sensitive, though, to these kids' feelings. If someone's parents recently divorced or if someone's parent recently died, you may want to talk with them about the game ahead of time.

Have the kids form two teams, and give each team a noisemaker. Explain that you're going to show a picture on the screen. The first team to sound its noisemaker will have the opportunity to begin bidding.

During bidding, the first team should say something like, "We can name that couple in three clues." Then the other team has the opportunity to say something like, "We can name that couple in two clues." The bidding continues until one of the teams wants the opposition to name the couple; at that point, the team says, "Name that couple." Then the other team must do so with as many clues from the clue cards as they bid on. Read the correct number of clues from the clue card, and then ask the team to name that couple. If the team answers correctly, it gets a point. If the team answers incorrectly, the opposing team gets a point.

Continue the game until teams have seen all the slides. The losing team, the team with the least points, must sing "Let Me Call You Sweetheart" or another love song to the winning team.

VARIATION

For extra fun, include slides of famous couples, and write clues for them. This way, the game won't get easier through the process of elimination.

As another idea, invite the parents to attend the meeting. Have the kids serve the parents dinner. Then have the parents watch and enjoy while the kids play the game. After the game, have the losing team sing to the parents.

SECRET PALS

Overview: Kids will get "secret pals" and find objects that represent good qualities about their pals.

Game Type: Affirmation, discussion-starter, suitable for disabled

Group Size: 10 to 20

Time Involved: 10 to 20 minutes

Supplies: A Bible, a hat or bag, slips of paper, a pen, and a watch

Preparation: On each slip of paper, write a group member's name. Then fold the slips of paper, and place them in the hat.

Have kids draw names from the hat. Explain that the person whose name they drew is their secret pal, so kids should keep the names a secret.

Say: **Your assignment for the next ten minutes is to look for an object somewhere in this meeting area that represents a good quality in your secret pal. Be prepared to present the object to your secret pal and explain to the group what good quality the object represents.**

Give kids ten minutes to find the objects. Then have kids form a circle for the presentation. Give each person a chance to describe why he or she chose the object—without revealing the secret pal's name. Then give kids a chance to guess who the secret pal might be. If kids guess the secret pal, have the person give the object to the secret pal. If kids don't guess the secret pal, have the person reveal the identity of the secret pal and present him or her with the object.

After every secret pal has received an object, read aloud 1 John 4:7.

Say: **Christ commands us to love one another. One of the best ways to do this is through gifts as you've done with this game. On Valentine's Day people who love each other profess their love, often with gifts. Though we have to put these objects back, you can keep the verbal gifts you received tonight as reminders that we love you. Remember that Christ loves you too.**

Ask:

● **What gifts can you give others every day?**
● **What changes would you see in our group if we did those things?**

TRIANGLE OF LOVE

Overview: Kids will act out roles to score points.

Game Type: Funny, no supplies and no preparation, quiet, suitable for disabled

Group Size: 20 to 30

Time Involved: 2 to 10 minutes

Supplies: None

Preparation: None

Have kids form two teams. Explain that teams will use three roles to play a group version of Rock, Paper, Scissors, in which the maiden beats the suitor, the suitor beats the preacher, and the preacher beats the maiden.

Each team will decide whether it will represent the coy maiden, the manly suitor, or the preacher. The coy maiden is represented by holding one finger under the chin and by twisting one foot back and forth. The manly suitor is represented by kneeling on one knee with one hand over the heart and the other outstretched. The preacher is represented by clasping hands together and nodding and smiling.

Before you give the signal to start, give teams a few moments to decide what they want to represent. The whole team must do the motion for the character it chooses to represent. The team that wins the round scores one point. The first team to score five points wins.

VARIATION

Add a brain-stretching element to this game by asking kids to predict, based on the law of averages, which representation will be most likely to occur.

PRESIDENTS DAY

PRESIDENTIAL TAG

Overview: Kids will play a variation of Tag in which only a presidential hero can free them.

Game Type: Active, no supplies and no preparation

Group Size: Any

Time Involved: 10 to 20 minutes

Supplies: None

Preparation: None

Choose a person to be "It." Whenever "It" tags someone, the person must freeze according to where he or she has been touched. If kids are tagged on the back, they must raise their arms above their heads and clasp hands to resemble the Washington monument. If kids are tagged on an arm, they must pretend to sit in a chair to resemble the Lincoln monument. If kids are tagged on a leg, they must get down on their hands and knees and round their backs to resemble the Jefferson monument.

Anyone who isn't tagged can "unfreeze" tagged people by tagging them and shouting, "I'm William Henry Harrison, and I've come to save you!" They can substitute the name of any president for William Henry Harrison.

When "It" wants to name another tagger to take over, "It" can shout, "Stop in the name of the Constitution!" and the next person he or she touches must become "It."

St. Patrick's Day

Leprechaun Laps

Overview: Kids will enjoy this variation of Duck, Duck, Goose.

Game Type: Active, no supplies and no preparation

Group Size: 10 to 20

Time Involved: 10 to 20 minutes

Supplies: None

Preparation: None

Have the group sit in a tight circle. This is a game to celebrate the "little people" of Ireland, so everyone who plays must appear to be very small. Choose one person to be the first leprechaun. This person must squat down and grasp his or her ankles and walk around behind the circle. He or she can release his or her ankles only to tap the shoulder of the person chosen to follow in hot pursuit. The chosen person must get up, assume the same position, and chase the leprechaun, trying to tag the leprechaun before he or she can take the spot left vacant. The person left semi-standing becomes the leprechaun in the next round.

PALM SUNDAY

FIND THE DONKEY

Overview: Kids will attempt to find a donkey or horse at the end of a treasure hunt.

Game Type: Bible, discussion-starter, suitable for disabled

Group Size: Any

Time Involved: 30 to 45 minutes

Supplies: A Bible, a donkey or horse, index cards, and a pen

Preparation: Arrange for kids to travel to four or five stops before reaching a destination where they'll find a donkey or horse. The final destination might be a zoo, park, or farm where a horse or donkey resides. Have a volunteer at each clue location to give kids the next clue. Write the clues on index cards, and deliver them to the proper locations. You may also want to recruit volunteers to drive the kids. These volunteers should know the clue locations and destinations in case kids can't figure out where they should go.

Have the kids form travel teams of four or five. Read Mark 11:1-10 to your group. Tell them they are going to experience a Palm Sunday treasure hunt. They will be given clues that will lead them eventually to a colt.

Show teams the index card with the first clue, and tell them you'll see them at the final destination.

At each location, have the volunteer show kids the next clue. When everyone has arrived at the final destination, discuss how the disciples must have felt to receive the instructions about the colt they were to find for Jesus that first Palm Sunday.

Hose-Anna

Overview: Kids will love this game of reverse limbo.

Game Type: Active, Bible, outside

Group Size: Any

Time Involved: 20 to 30 minutes

Supplies: One garden hose that's attached to itself to form a circle

Preparation: None

Say: **In Mark 11 we read about the first Palm Sunday. Jesus sent two of his disciples to Bethphage to find a colt that had never been ridden before and to bring the colt to him.**

For our game today, I need a volunteer to play the part of this famous colt that we'll call "Anna." Now I need the rest of the group to hold onto the hose while Anna stands in the middle of the circle. The game is played like a reverse version of the limbo. We'll start by holding the hose at knee height and see if Anna can get out of the corral without touching the hose. Each time Anna clears the hose without touching it, we'll raise the hose six inches. When the hose reaches chest height, Anna can use the disciples holding the hose as steps for climbing over the hose. But the disciples must keep both hands on the hose at all times.

Don't let the hose get above shoulder height for safety purposes. Be sure that everyone who wants to try the part of "Anna" gets a chance.

LEADER TIP

If you have aggressive, high-jumping players in your group, make sure you have some cushions and spotters on the other side of the hose to help catch them when they jump.

PALM RACE

Overview: Kids will race with partners using leftover palm branches.

Game Type: Active, funny

Group Size: Any

Time Involved: 2 to 10 minutes

Supplies: Palm branches, index cards, a pen, masking tape, and a hat or box. If your church uses real palm branches for a Palm Sunday service, ask if your group can use the leftovers.

Preparation: Write each of the following body parts on two index cards: elbow, knee, finger, nose, thumb, wrist, shoulder, head, and eye. Place the cards in a hat. Mark a short obstacle course with masking tape.

Have kids form even-numbered teams. If you have an uneven number of kids, either join a team, or ask one player to go twice.

Hand the first two players from each team one palm branch. Then pull two index cards out of the hat. The two players from each team must carry the palm branch through the course and race the pairs from the other teams. However, pairs may touch the palm branch only with the body parts listed on the cards you draw from the box. After you've read the cards to the pairs, put the cards back in the hat, and mix them up.

If a pair drops the branch or touches it with anything other than the designated body parts, that pair must start over. Have pairs race to see who can finish first. Then have the next set of pairs go. The team in which the most pairs finish first wins.

PRAISE PALMS

Overview: Kids will encourage each other with palm leaves of praise.

Game Type: Active, affirmation, suitable for disabled

Group Size: Any

Time Involved: 10 to 20 minutes

Supplies: A Bible, green construction paper, scissors, and pencils

Preparation: None

LEADER TIP

You may want to provide tape so kids can tape their palm leaves together as sort of miniature palm trees to keep.

Have kids sit in a circle, and distribute green construction paper, pencils, and scissors. Have each person cut a palm branch from the paper, and be sure kids cut the same number of leaves as there are group members.

Explain that group members will be writing words of praise about each other. Ask kids to write the name of every other group member on a palm leaf. Then ask kids to write something positive about each person on the other side of the palm leaf.

After several minutes, ask the group to form two lines about five feet apart, with lines facing each other. Explain that each group member will "ride through Jerusalem" as Jesus did on Palm Sunday. Read aloud Matthew 21:1-10. Then enlist one person to serve as the "donkey" for a few "riders." Though kids can simply walk through the middle of the lines, it's much funnier if they ride through.

Have each group member take a turn "riding" through the lines. As each rider passes, kids standing in the lines tear off the palm leaf with that person's name and toss it at the rider. As kids toss the leaves, they must shout

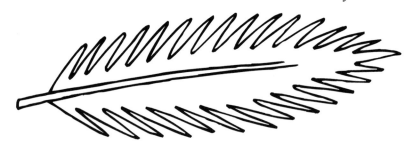

out the words of praise they wrote down about the rider.

When the rider has finished riding through the lines, he or she should hop off the donkey and collect the leaves from the floor. The donkey can rest or hurry back to carry another person. Continue until everyone has had the chance to be the rider.

GOOD FRIDAY

CARRYING THE CROSS

Overview: Kids will experience a simulation of the role of Simon
from Cyrene.

Game Type: Active, Bible

Group Size: Any

Time Involved: 2 to 10 minutes

Supplies: A Bible

Preparation: None

Say: **In Matthew 27:32 we read about a critical player in the true
drama that we celebrate today as Good Friday.**

Read aloud the verse, and then say: **You're going to run a relay race
that will help you experience this aspect of the Good Friday story in a
new way.**

Have kids form two even teams, and have teams line up at one end of the
room. Then have teammates form pairs with someone of similar height and
weight.

Say: **For the relay you'll stand back to back with your partner. The
players facing the starting line will pick up their partners behind them by
hooking arms and leaning forward with the other person on their back.**

Continue: **Once you have hoisted your partner in the air and I start the race, you will run to the other end of the room, trade places with your partner, and then run back. As soon as one pair returns, the next pair may start.**

Start the game. The team that finishes first wins.

CRISSCROSS

Overview: Kids will walk blindfolded, guided by directions from other players.

Game Type: Suitable for disabled

Group Size: 2 to 10

Time Involved: 10 to 20 minutes

Supplies: Blindfolds, a watch, and masking tape

Preparation: Use masking tape to create a cross diagram on the floor.

Gather kids in the center of the room. Explain that each person is going to try to walk from one end of the room to the other while blindfolded. Add that the only way to get to the other side is by listening to the directions given by other players positioned along the room's walls.

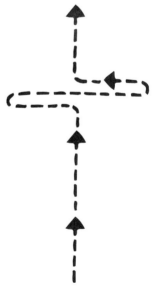

Explain that starting at the center of one wall, a blindfolded player must move across the floor in a large cross pattern. The player must stay on top of or as close to the masking tape cross as possible, and other kids must shout instructions to help blindfolded players do so. Players straying too far from the line must return to the start. The blindfolded player must reach the other side of the room and touch the wall.

Select and blindfold a volunteer. Place everyone else around the room, covering all the walls as much as possible. Have everyone take a turn, and time each person. The person who finishes fastest wins.

CROSS-CARRY RELAY

Overview: Kids will run a relay to symbolize Good Friday.

Game Type: Bible, discussion-starter

Group Size: 10 to 20

Time Involved: 10 to 20 minutes

Supplies: Twenty-five-pound bags of potatoes, bread, juice, cups, a plate, chocolate kisses, and bandannas or scarves

Preparation: Set up five different stations. At the first station, the designated starting place, place a bag of potatoes for each team of five. At the second station, arrange a plate of bread and small cups of juice. At the third station, place a bag of chocolate kisses. At the fourth station, place the bandannas.

Have kids form teams of five. Explain that teams will do a relay that symbolizes what Christ went through on what we call Good Friday. Here's how the relay works: One person from each team should stand at each station. The kids at the designated starting place each should pick up a bag of potatoes, which represents the weight of the cross Christ had to carry, and drag or carry it to the second station. When the kids at the second station are tagged by their team members, they should eat the bread and drink the juice to represent the Last Supper. When they've completely swallowed the bread and juice, they each should pick up the bag of potatoes and go to the third station. When the kids at the third station are tagged, they each should unwrap and eat a chocolate kiss to represent the identifying kiss Judas gave Jesus. When they've completely swallowed the chocolate kiss, they each should pick up the bag of potatoes and go to the fourth station. When kids at the fourth station are tagged, they each should wrap a bandanna around their heads to represent the crown of thorns. After they've tied the bandannas, they each should pick up the bag of potatoes and take it to the fifth

LEADER TIP You may want to have the kids choose a shelter to deliver the bags of potatoes to.	station. When the kids at the fifth station are tagged, they each should crow like a rooster three times, pick up the bag of potatoes, and take it back to the starting place.

After the relay, discuss the game's symbols with the kids.

Good Friday Word Search

Overview: Kids will create words from letters on their backs.

Game Type: Mixer, quiet, suitable for disabled

Group Size: 10 to 20

Time Involved: 2 to 10 minutes

Supplies: Tape, paper, a marker, and pens

Preparation: Write the letters of the following words on separate sheets of paper: Friday, burial, stone. For example, you'll have a sheet of paper with an "F" on it, a sheet with an "r" on it, and so on. If you have more than seventeen players, add other words that relate to Good Friday.

Have kids form two teams, and then tape a letter to every person's back. Give each team a sheet of paper and a pen, and tell them to create words from the letters on each other's backs. Explain that each word they write counts as one point, but words relating to Good Friday count as five points.

Give teams about five minutes to list as many words as they can and then tally the points. The team with the highest score wins.

Here are some examples of words kids can form from the letters:

Friday	Stone	Burial
day	nose	rub
rid	tone	lab
fir	son	bar
ray	ton	bur
fray	not	ail
fad	toes	rail
rad	one	bail
far	on	lair
raid	nest	rib
	notes	liar

PASSOVER

EGYPTIANS AND JEWS

Overview: Kids will race through an obstacle course.

Game Type: Bible, discussion-starter, outside, team-builder

Group Size: Any

Time Involved: 10 to 20 minutes

Supplies: Scissors, heavy string or shoelaces

Preparation: Cut lengths of string so they're long enough for kids to tie around their ankles. Create a simple, flat obstacle course outside that's about twenty yards long. For example, direct kids to walk around a tree and under a volleyball net.

Have kids form two teams, the Egyptians and the Jews. Explain that the team that races through the course first wins. The catch is that teammates will be tied together at the ankles.

Distribute string, and have kids tie their ankles together. Then start the race. After both teams have finished, summarize the story of the Jewish flight from Egypt. Lead kids into a discussion of how the Jews worked together to escape from the Egyptians.

EASTER

BREAK AN EGG

Overview: Kids will challenge each other to see who's got the strongest egg.

Game Type: Messy, mixer, outside, suitable for disabled

Group Size: Any

Time Involved: 10 to 20 minutes

Supplies: Hard-boiled eggs

Preparation: None

Distribute hard-boiled eggs, and explain that kids will see who has the strongest egg. Explain that the narrower end of the egg is the "nose" and the wider end of the egg is the "noggin."

Say: **If you think you've got a good egg, challenge someone to an egg battle. That person must then hold out his or her egg with the nose facing out. The challenger must then use the nose of his or her egg to hit the nose of the other person's egg. If your hit cracks the other person's egg, he or she must hold out the egg with the noggin facing out, and the challenger must hit the noggin with the noggin of his or her own egg. If the other person's egg cracks again, the challenger gets to keep both eggs. If, with either hit, the other person's egg doesn't crack, that person gets the challenger's egg. And be careful, because if you knock the egg so hard that it falls out of the person's hand, you have to surrender your egg to that person.**

Encourage kids to figure out how best to hold their eggs to receive hits and how best to hit other eggs. The person who ends up with the most eggs wins the game.

CONE EGG

Overview: Kids will attempt to remove objects placed beneath a speed cone without breaking an egg.

Game Type: Active, messy, outside, suitable for disabled

Group Size: 2 to 10

Time Involved: 2 to 10 minutes

Supplies: Six small speed cones; six raw eggs; a watch; paper towels; and six objects small enough to hide beneath a speed235 cone, such as a ball, eraser, pencil, paper cup, jump rope, or wash cloth

Preparation: Set the cones several yards apart. Place one object beneath each cone, making sure the object is completely hidden. Set one egg on top of each cone.

Explain that kids are going on a special Easter egg hunt.

Say: **One person at a time will try to remove items hidden beneath the speed cones. Everyone should avoid breaking the eggs placed on top. Your goal is to remove all six items in the shortest time possible without breaking any eggs. Though you may use both hands, you can't touch, steady, or balance an egg at any time. If an egg falls unbroken, ten seconds will be added to your time. If an egg breaks, twenty seconds will be added. The player with the shortest total time is the winner.**

Start the game, and record each player's time. After everyone has raced, declare a winner.

EASTER CHEER HUNT

Overview: Kids will spread the good news that Jesus is alive.

Game Type: Service, suitable for disabled

Group Size: Any

Time Involved: More than 1 hour

Supplies: Bags of individually wrapped Easter candies

Preparation: Recruit volunteers to drive kids around town.

Have kids form groups based on vehicle loads. Give each group a bag of candy, and challenge them to get rid of their candy the fastest—without eating it!

Say: **Many people in our community don't get to celebrate Easter as we do because they have to work. So we're going to attempt to bring some Easter cheer into their lives. You must deliver pieces of candy to employees of different businesses around town. You can give someone only one piece of candy, and you must tell each person that Jesus is alive. Remember, deliver the candy to employees who are working today. The first team to deliver all the candy and come back here wins.**

Suggest that kids visit gas stations, grocery stores, movie theaters, restaurants, hospitals, nursing homes, and hotels.

EASTER EGG ASSEMBLY LINE

Overview: Kids will form a human conveyor belt and race to dye a dozen eggs.

Game Type: Active, messy, outside

Group Size: 20 to 30

Time Involved: 10 to 20 minutes

Supplies: Two dozen hard-boiled eggs, two egg cartons, two cups of egg dye, two spoons or egg dippers, and heavy-duty paper towels

Preparation: For each team, place a dozen eggs at the starting line and the egg dye, spoons, and egg cartons at the finish line.

Have kids form two teams, and then have teammates form pairs. Give each pair a paper towel. Then have each team form a vertical line stretching across the playing area toward the finish line, with pairs standing about two feet from each other. The partners in each pair should each be holding two corners of the paper towel between them.

On your cue, the first pairs in each line should place an egg on their paper towel, raise it up, and carry it over the heads of the rest of their teammates.

When they reach the end of the line, they must dunk the egg into the cup of dye, remove it, and place it into the egg carton to dry. Meanwhile, the rest of their team takes a sideways step toward the starting line so the second pair in each team can load their egg. The first pair assumes the last position in the line. Play continues until the teams have dyed all dozen eggs. Declare the team to finish first the winner.

Have the eggs for a snack, or donate your efforts to a children's egg hunt.

EGG ROLLING

Overview: Kids will see who can roll an egg the fastest.

Game Type: Active, outside

Group Size: Any

Time Involved: 2 to 10 minutes

Supplies: Eggs

Preparation: None

In an open space, have kids line up shoulder to shoulder and then move apart so there's about two feet of space between each person and the next. Give each person an egg, and explain that kids will race to see who can push an egg the fastest—using only their noses. Stand about fifty feet in front of the kids at the finish line, and shout: **Ready? Go!** The person who crosses the finish line first, pushing the egg along only with his or her nose, wins.

MARSHMALLOW MADNESS

Overview: Kids will try to feed marshmallow chicks to each other.

Game Type: Food, funny, messy, suitable for disabled

Group Size: Any

Time Involved: 2 to 10 minutes

Supplies: Marshmallow chicks, blindfolds, cups, and water

Preparation: Fill cups with water.

Have kids form two teams. Have each team form two equal lines, facing each other from opposite ends of the room.

Blindfold the first player in each line, and give him or her a marshmallow chick. At your starting signal, blindfolded players should try to walk across the room toward their partners and then feed their partners the marshmallow chicks. Team members may call out directions to their blindfolded players. Players must thoroughly chew the marshmallow treats before removing the blindfolds and rushing back to the next player in line, who will repeat the process. Players should sit down after their turns. The first team with all players seated wins.

Be sure to caution kids about choking hazards, and be standing by with water.

> **VARIATION**
>
> Use this game for Valentine's Day by substituting marshmallow hearts.

PUTTING ALL YOUR EGGS IN ONE BASKET—OR NOT!

Overview: Kids will participate in an Easter egg hunt that requires strategy and negotiating skills.

Game Type: Food, mixer, suitable for disabled

Group Size: 10 to 20

Time Involved: 10 to 20 minutes

Supplies: A watch; Starburst candies; other assorted, wrapped Easter candies, such as chocolate eggs and colored sugar eggs; plastic cups to serve as Easter baskets; and a small prize, such as a stuffed chick or a chocolate bunny

Preparation: Hide the candy for an Easter egg hunt, but keep one Starburst candy of each color.

Give each player a cup, and tell kids they have a few minutes to find as many hidden candies as they can. After the allotted time, say:

I have placed one Starburst candy of each color in a cup. In a few minutes, I'll choose one of those colors of Starburst, and whoever has the most Starburst candies of that color will win a prize. In the meantime, everyone may trade and strike deals, negotiating to accumulate Starburst candies. For example, you might try to amass Starburst candies of just one color, hoping that color will be the one I choose. Or you might try to acquire equal amounts of all colors of Starburst candies. Or you may decide to keep what you have and take your chances!

You can also use the other kinds of candy to negotiate deals. Or you can forego the competition all together, "selling" your Starburst candies in order to acquire your personal favorite types of candy. Use your imagination! You have five minutes.

Call time after five minutes, and blindly draw one of the Starburst candies from your cup. Award the prize to the person with the most Starburst candies of that color, and ask the winner to share his or her strategy.

RISE AGAIN

Overview: Kids will work together to stand up in groups of growing numbers.

Game Type: Active, no supplies and no preparation

Group Size: 30 to 50

Time Involved: 2 to 10 minutes

Supplies: None

Preparation: None

Have kids form teams of ten, and have teammates form pairs.

Say: **Please sit down back to back with your partner. Now try to stand up as a team with your elbows locked.**

Once everyone has mastered this move, have pairs form foursomes and try to stand up together. Keep adding pairs until all ten team members can stand up together in this unusual way.

TASTE AND SEE

Overview: Kids will race to figure out candy flavors.

Game Type: Food, suitable for disabled

Group Size: Any

Time Involved: 2 to 10 minutes

Supplies: Individually wrapped Easter candies in different flavors and small paper bags

Preparation: Put different flavors of Easter candy into several bags.

Have kids form teams of six, and have each team line up single file. Explain that kids are going to race to find out which team has the keenest sense of taste for candy flavors.

Say: **The first person in line will turn to the second person in line. The second person in line will close his or her eyes while the first person feeds the second person a piece of candy. As soon as the second person accurately names the candy's flavor, he or she will repeat the process with the third person in line. When the last person in line has guessed correctly, he or she will feed the first person in line. When everyone on the team has guessed correctly, sit down. The team that sits down first wins.**

Mother's Day

Mom for a Day

Overview: Kids will pretend to be moms doing chores.

Game Type: Active, discussion-starter, funny, no supplies and no preparation, suitable for disabled

Group Size: Any

Time Involved: 10 to 20 minutes

Supplies: None

Preparation: None

Have kids form groups of six, and explain that each group member will get a chance to play "mom." Group members should decide who will be the mom; the other group members need to stand as still as mannequins. You'll call out a chore or duty, and each group's designated mom will need to transform the motionless group members into an inanimate object, such as a desk, washing machine, refrigerator, computer, or car. Once the mom has moved and bent and configured the group members to be the inanimate object needed, he or she should pretend to perform the chore or duty, including speaking as if performing that duty. For example, if you call out "carpooling," a mom could transform group members into a "car" and then pretend to drive the car while saying, "Hop in! We'll just pick up two more people and then head to soccer practice."

When everyone understands, call out the first chore. Some possibilities include doing the family's budget, working at the office, washing clothes, buying groceries, coaching a team sport, and so on. When all the groups are acting out that chore, have kids switch roles. Then call out a new chore. Continue until everyone has had a chance to be the mom.

LEADER TIP

As with any game about specific family members, use sensitivity during these games. Some kids' mothers live elsewhere, and some have died. Encourage kids to think about either their real mothers or an older woman they trust. Avoid alienating kids by naming specific mothers or by pointing out their situations. Finally, if kids don't want to participate, don't force them to.

Afterward, ask:

- What was it like to be "mom" for a day?
- How many duties do moms perform on a regular basis?
- What does this game tell you about what moms do?
- What are some things we can do to show our moms how much we appreciate them?

MOM'S BRAG BOUQUET

Overview: Kids will share positive memories of their moms.

Game Type: Quiet, service, suitable for disabled

Group Size: 2 to 10

Time Involved: 10 to 20 minutes

Supplies: Ribbon, markers, colorful construction paper, scissors, and hole punches

Preparation: None

Have kids sit in a circle, and place the supplies in the middle of the circle. Ask kids to think back as far as possible for a memory involving their mother. Ask if anyone has a "mom" memory from when he or she was one, two, three, and so on, until the present. Stress that this is not a competitive game, but one that shows the importance of mother's influence in their lives.

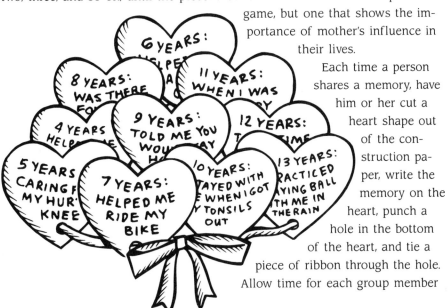

Each time a person shares a memory, have him or her cut a heart shape out of the construction paper, write the memory on the heart, punch a hole in the bottom of the heart, and tie a piece of ribbon through the hole. Allow time for each group member

to share a memory from each year. Afterward, have each person group together his or her construction paper hearts and tie them together with ribbon to form a bouquet of memories to give to Mom.

A Mother's Work Is Never Done

Overview: Kids will remember the things Mom does.

Game Type: Discussion-starter, quiet, suitable for disabled

Group Size: Any

Time Involved: 10 to 20 minutes

Supplies: A watch, pencils, paper, and a collection of items that reflect what moms do—for example, a checkbook, an oil can, cooking utensils, a thimble, car keys, garden tools, calendars, an apron, clothes pins, a music book, baby rattles, a screwdriver, jogging shoes, a box of Girl Scout cookies, cleaning supplies, a thermometer, a Bible, a coach's whistle, and a box of tissues

Preparation: Recruit a woman to play the "mom." Have the mom place all the items you collected on her person. She can layer items or use other props, such as an apron or a bucket, to carry them, but all the items must be visible.

Have kids form pairs. Have "mom" walk into the room, displaying all the items. After five minutes, have her leave.

Say: **That mom represented many moms. She was carrying items that represent the many things moms do. With your partner, list as many things as you can that our model mom was wearing, and include what they might represent. You'll get one point for each item and one point for what it represents. The pair with the most points after five minutes wins.**

After five minutes, call time. Have pairs write their names on their papers and then switch papers with another pair. Then ask the model mom to come back in. Go over each item and what it might represent, and have pairs add up points on their papers.

Afterward, lead your kids into a discussion about mothers' roles in their kids' lives. Ask:

- **How can we more often show our mothers that we appreciate them?**

MEMORIAL DAY

REMEMBRANCE

Overview: Kids will play a trivia game they create themselves.

Game Type: Knowledge-builder, quiet, suitable for disabled

Group Size: 30 to 50

Time Involved: 20 to 30 minutes

Supplies: Paper, pens, and small U.S. flags (from craft stores)

Preparation: None

Have kids form teams of six, and assign each team a number. Distribute paper and pencils to each team, and have teams write down as many facts as they can remember about a few major U.S. military conflicts—the American Revolution, Civil War, World War I, and World War II.

After about five minutes, collect the fact sheets; be sure each team's number is on its sheet.

Give each team a small flag, and begin the questioning. Use each fact teams wrote down (unless you know it to be inaccurate), forming the fact into a question. For example, if a team wrote that the Declaration of Independence was signed in 1776, you could ask, "In what year was the Declaration of Independence signed?" All teams except the one that wrote the fact can try to answer. If a team wants to answer, it should raise its flag. The first team to do so gets the first opportunity to answer. If the team answers incorrectly, the second team to hold up a flag can try.

If a team answers correctly, it gets ten points. If a team answers incorrectly, deduct ten points from its score. If no one can correctly answer the question, the team that wrote the fact gets ten points. You can either play until you've read all the facts or until a team reaches one hundred points.

Here are some example questions for each conflict:

American Revolution

1) When did the American colonies adopt the Declaration of Independence? (July 4, 1776)

2) What country ruled the American colonies in 1776? (Great Britain)

3) Who was commander-in-chief of the American military during the American Revolution? (George Washington)

4) Who rode from Boston to Lexington to warn colonists of the advancing British army? (Paul Revere)

Civil War

1) In what year did the Civil War begin? (1861)

2) What did the Emancipation Proclamation do? (Freed all slaves)

3) Who was president during the Civil War? (Abraham Lincoln)

4) What two entities fought in the Civil War? (The Union and the Confederacy)

World War I

1) On what side did the United States fight in World War I? (Allies)

2) Who was the U.S. president during WW I? (Woodrow Wilson)

3) Which country, mainly, did the U.S. fight against in World War I? (Germany)

4) What treaty ended World War I? (Treaty of Versailles)

World War II

1) Who was president of the U.S. during WW II? (Franklin Roosevelt)

2) Why did the U.S. become involved in the war? (Japan bombed Pearl Harbor.)

3) Who was the German leader during World War II? (Adolf Hitler)

4) Which countries were the U.S.'s three greatest allies during WW II? (France, the Soviet Union, and Great Britain)

Flag Day

You're a Grand Old Chair—I Mean Flag

Overview: Kids will enjoy celebrating Flag Day with this relay race.

Game Type: Active, funny, outside

Group Size: Any

Time Involved: 2 to 10 minutes

Supplies: Two sturdy flags (Decorative holiday flags work well and prevent your group from desecrating our national flag.)

Preparation: None

Have kids form two teams. Designate a starting line and a finish line about thirty feet apart from each other.

Say: **In honor of Flag Day, we'll have a relay race using the flag. Get into groups of three within your teams. Two people will hold each end of the flag, and the third person will sit in the middle of the flag. At my signal, your group will run down to the finish line and then run back. If the person sitting on the flag falls down, you must stop and get that person back on the flag before you can keep going.**

Start the game. The team that finishes first wins.

Father's Day

LEADER TIP

As with any game about specific family members, use sensitivity during these games. Some kids' fathers live elsewhere, and some have died. Encourage kids to think about either their real fathers or an older man they trust. Avoid alienating kids by naming specific fathers or by pointing out their situations. Finally, if kids don't want to participate, don't force them to.

Father Knows Best

Overview: Kids will play a variation of the game Simon Says.

Type of Game: Discussion-starter, no supplies and no preparation, suitable for disabled

Group Size: Any

Time Involved: 2 to 10 minutes

Supplies: None

Preparation: None

Have kids line up shoulder to shoulder at one end of your meeting area, keeping some open space behind them so they can walk backward.

Say: **We're going to play a game called Father Says to celebrate Father's Day. We'll play it like the Simon Says game, but with a few new twists. I'll start a statement with "Father Says" and complete it by giving you an action. For example, I might say, "Father says to bend over and touch your right foot with you right hand." I'll then follow that with another quick "Father says" statement that will have another action. You are to do the actions as quickly as possible. If I ever tell you to do an action without first saying "Father Says" and you do it, you will take one step backward. When only one person is standing on our original line, that person will become the Father and take my place.**

Play the game, giving the commands as quickly as possible. Here are some commands that you can add your own ideas to:

- Father says to jump up and down.
- Father says to tap your head with your right hand.
- Father says to squat down.
- Stand up. (If someone does this, he or she should take a step backward.)
- Father says to rub your neighbor's back.

- Father says to touch your nose.
- Touch your ear. (If someone does this, he or she should take a step backward.)
- Father says to blink your eyes.
- Father says to grab both ears.
- Father says to cover your eyes.
- Put your hands on your shoulders. (If someone does this, he or she should take a step backward.)

After the game, ask:

- **What are some of the things your dad tells you to do that you don't like to do?**
- **What do you like most about your dad?**
- **What's one question you'd like to ask your dad?**
- **What has been the best time you've ever had with your dad?**

King of the Hat

Overview: Kids will collect hats during a relay.

Game Type: Active, discussion-starter, funny

Group Size: 10 to 20

Time Involved: 2 to 10 minutes

Supplies: Large sheets of construction paper or newsprint, masking tape, and a marker

Preparation: Make several hats out of construction paper or newsprint. Use tape to secure the paper hats.

Have kids sit in a circle, and ask:

- **What are some different "hats" fathers wear?**

As kids respond, write each job on a different paper hat. After all the hats are labeled, place them at one end of the room. Have the kids form a single-file line at the end of the room opposite the hats. Explain that the group is going to run a relay in which the goal is to add hats along the way.

The first player rushes across the room and picks up any hat. He or she puts on the hat and rushes back to the group to tag the second player. The second player takes the first hat, puts it on, runs across the floor, and puts on another hat. That player rushes back to the group to tag the third player without dropping either hat.

This pattern continues until a player is wearing all the hats. It will be practically impossible to carry all the hats without dropping at least one. When someone drops a hat, the player must say something he or she appreciates about a father figure—for example, "He always tries to keep his word." Then the player moves to end of the line, and the next player takes his or her place.

After the relay, ask:

- **What was challenging about this activity?**
- **Was there anything rewarding about the game?**
- **What was it like to lose your place and move to the back of the line?**
- **How difficult do you think it is for fathers to wear so many "hats" so often?**
- **Is it possible for you to wear some of your father's hats? Explain.**

SHAVING "DAD"

Overview: Kids will practice shaving with whipped cream and graham crackers.

Game Type: Food, funny, messy, suitable for disabled

Group Size: Any

Time Involved: 2 to 10 minutes

Supplies: Small plates, whipped cream, graham crackers, napkins, a spoon, trash bags, scissors, and blindfolds

Preparation: You'll need a plate of whipped cream and one section of a graham cracker for every four kids. Put about a half cup of whipped cream on each plate.

Have kids form teams of four and choose one team member to be the dad, one to be the coach, one to be the applier, and one to be the shaver. Have the dads each cut a neck hole in a trash bag and then put on the trash bag.

Then have the dads take a plate of whipped cream and a section of graham cracker and spread out in a line at one end of the area. Have each team line up opposite its dad at the other end of the room. Ask the coaches to help the appliers and shavers put on blindfolds.

Say: **This is how the game will work. The coach will spin the applier and then, without using hands, will help the applier get to the dad at the other end of the room. Then the applier must apply whipped cream to the dad's face as if it's shaving cream. Again, the coach can only use words to help direct the applier. Then, with the coach's verbal help, the applier must walk back to tag the shaver, who will then use the coach's verbal help to get to the dad and use the graham cracker to "shave" the dad.**

When everyone understands, signal the start of the game. While the main purpose of the game is to have fun, a team can win based on how fast and how thoroughly it shaves the dad.

If you have time, let kids switch roles and play again.

INDEPENDENCE DAY

"AMERICA THE BEAUTIFUL" VIDEO SHOW

Overview: Kids will videotape beautiful things about the U.S.

Game Type: Outside, senior high, suitable for disabled

Group Size: 2 to 10

Time Involved: More than 1 hour

Supplies: Camcorders with blank videotapes, the "America the Beautiful" handout (p. 252), a TV, and a VCR. Ask church members to loan their camcorders to the group for a day.

Preparation: Make photocopies of the "America the Beautiful" handout (p. 252). Recruit volunteers to drive the kids around town.

Have kids form groups to fit in the vehicles. Give each group an "America the Beautiful" handout (p. 252). Explain that groups will use camcorders to videotape people, places, and things that represent the lyrics to the song. Tell kids they have one hour to create their video and return. Remind kids to be very careful with the equipment.

When kids return, watch the videos they created. You may want each group to sing the song "America the Beautiful" during its video for extra fun.

Use the lyrics from the following song to help you choose what to include in your video.

America the Beautiful

Katharine Lee Bates

O beautiful for spacious skies,
For amber waves of grain,
For purple mountain majesties
Above the fruited plain!
America! America!
God shed his grace on thee
And crown thy good with brotherhood
From sea to shining sea!
O beautiful for pilgrim feet
Whose stern, impassioned stress
A thoroughfare for freedom beat
Across the wilderness!
America! America!
God mend thine every flaw,
Confirm thy soul in self-control,
Thy liberty in law.
O beautiful for heroes proved
In liberating strife,
Who more than self the country loved
And mercy more than life!
America! America!
May God thy gold refine
Till all success be nobleness
And every gain divine!
O beautiful for patriot dream
That sees beyond the years
Thine alabaster cities gleam
Undimmed by human tears!
America! America!
God shed his grace on thee
And crown thy good with brotherhood
From sea to shining sea.

CRACKERS!

Overview: Kids will create their own fireworks by chewing up and spitting out crackers.

Game Type: Food, funny, messy, outside, suitable for disabled

Group Size: Any

Time Involved: 2 to 10 minutes

Supplies: Crackers and wet wipes

Preparation: None

Have kids stand in a circle outside. Give each person five crackers. Explain that the group is going to take part in some fireworks by chewing the crackers and spitting them high into the air. Players should think of some crazy sound effects or body motions to add to the moment. Possible effects include humming, buzzing, stomping, or clapping. Possible body motions include spinning, hopping, jumping up and down on one foot, and waving the arms.

Explain that you want to group to celebrate Independence Day with a bang (and a mess!). Ask players to start chewing their crackers. Give a signal, and watch the "fireworks" fly! Forget about staying clean for this one, because crackers are going to land everywhere.

I DECLARE

Overview: Kids will make and sign a class "declaration" of purpose.

Game Type: Bible, discussion-starter, quiet, suitable for disabled, team-builder

Group Size: 10 to 20

Time Involved: 30 to 45 minutes

Supplies: Bibles, a dictionary, newsprint, tape, and markers

Preparation: None

Ask two volunteers to look up the words "declaration" and "independence" in the dictionary and then read aloud the definitions. Have kids discuss the meanings of these words and the ways the U.S. has followed or strayed from the words' meanings. Also have kids discuss the importance of countries having guidelines and goals.

Distribute Bibles, and have kids find Bible passages that the group could use as its guiding "declaration" or purpose—either short-term or long-term. Here are some possibilities you may want to share with the group:

- Serving others (Colossians 3:24; Ephesians 6:7)
- Praying regularly (2 Chronicles 7:14; James 5:13)
- Reaching out to less fortunate people (Matthew 6:4; Proverbs 28:27)
- Inviting people to church (John 1:8; Acts 1:8)

Tape a sheet of newsprint to a wall, and have the kids write their ideas on the newsprint. Then have kids vote on one declaration to concentrate on in the next few months. Ask kids to brainstorm for actions that support the declaration. Finally, ask group members to sign their own "John Hancock" near the bottom of the newsprint.

Keep the declaration in a prominent place in the meeting room as a reminder.

STATUE OF LIBERTY

Overview: Kids will decorate each other as the Statue of Liberty.

Game Type: Funny, suitable for disabled

Group Size: Any

Time Involved: 10 to 20 minutes

Supplies: A cassette player or CD player; a cassette tape or CD of patriotic songs; sheets or large, gray plastic trash bags; cardboard; scissors; markers; small plastic flags; and other supplies that students can use to decorate a teammate as the Statue of Liberty

Preparation: None

Explain to kids that the object of this game is for students to use their creativity to dress up a teammate to compete for the "Best-Looking Statue of Liberty" award.

Have kids form groups of five to eight. Ask each group to choose one person to be the Statue of Liberty. Give each team an equal amount of supplies, and encourage kids to use their creativity to decorate their Statue of Liberty.

Give teams about ten to fifteen minutes to prepare, and then play the Independence Day music loudly. Have the statues parade around the area as in a fashion show. Have kids cheer for their favorite statue. Give small flags to the winning team as prizes.

Success Always Begins With a Thought

Overview: Kids will guess how significant accomplishments got started.

Game Type: Discussion-starter, quiet, suitable for disabled

Group Size: Any

Time Involved: 20 to 30 minutes

Supplies: Pens and paper

Preparation: None

Distribute paper and pens. Have each player write down a significant recent accomplishment—earning a place on a sports team, winning a seat on the student council, acting in a play, or saving money for something important, for example. Underneath that accomplishment, each player should write about the first time he or she thought, Hey, I can do this. After kids have finished writing, collect their papers.

Shuffle the pages, and pass them around so each player gets a different person's paper. Ask for volunteers to read the accomplishments aloud without identifying the original author. After each accomplishment, have kids guess the circumstances surrounding the beginning of the idea.

Lead kids into a discussion to emphasize that the war for independence wasn't completed until the mid-1780s, but that's not what we celebrate. Instead, we celebrate July 4, 1776, when the idea of American independence was first germinated. Discuss the importance not only of ideas, but of choosing the ideas to follow through with.

LABOR DAY

THE WORST JOBS EVER

Overview: Kids will consider the world's worst jobs.

Game Type: Funny, no supplies and no preparation, quiet, suitable for disabled, travel

Group Size: 2 to 10

Time Involved: 2 to 10 minutes

Supplies: None

Preparation: None

To celebrate Labor Day, what could be more appropriate than thinking about working—working the world's worst jobs, that is.

Ask kids to each decide what would be the worst job they can think of. Suggest several ideas to prime their imaginations: a mosquito repellent tester, a dog food taster, a quality control test rider for roller coasters, for example.

Give the kids one minute to fix in their minds the jobs they think are among the world's worst, even if they aren't sure the jobs exist.

After a minute, say:

> **Now let's see if we can identify what our friends are thinking. Each of us will have a turn answering up to fifteen yes-or-no questions. At the end of fifteen questions, we'll have the opportunity to guess the job and see how close we are to identifying it.**

Give everyone a turn answering questions about the jobs they've identified as among the world's worst.

Columbus Day

Call Me Columbus

Overview: Kids will play a land version of the pool game Marco Polo.

Game Type: Active, outside

Group Size: Any

Time Involved: 10 to 20 minutes

Supplies: A blindfold

Preparation: None

Choose four people to represent the corners of the play area and one person to be "Christopher." Blindfold Christopher, and explain that his or her job is to tag someone else, making that person Christopher. In order to know where people are, he or she must call "Christopher," to which everyone must respond, "Columbus!" Each time someone else becomes "Christopher," restrict the play area by having the corners move in two steps. Have different students represent the corners after every couple of new Christophers so everyone gets a chance to play. To warn Christopher that he or she is wandering toward the edge of the play area, players can call out, "Storm approaching!" If Christopher moves outside the play area, stop play, bring him or her back to the center of the area, and start again. Continue playing until the area is too small for the group size.

Halloween

Mask Mixer

Overview: Kids will wear masks to pretend to be biblical characters.

Game Type: Bible, funny, suitable for disabled

Group Size: Any

Time Involved: 10 to 20 minutes

Supplies: Bibles, Bible commentaries, poster board, scissors, markers, and yarn

Preparation: Place all the materials on a table near the entrance to the area.

Try this as a fun alternative for your next Halloween celebration. As participants enter, direct them to the worktable near the entrance.

Ask everyone to research the Bibles and commentaries for biblical characters who would work well as masks. Possible characters include Eve, Noah, Moses, Deborah, Samson, Esther, Jesus, and Judas. Have kids use the supplies to create masks that symbolize the nature or personality of the characters. For example, an Eve mask could be red and shaped like an apple; a Noah mask could be rainbow-colored with a boat on the top and bottom; a Moses mask could include five commandments on each cheek; a Deborah mask

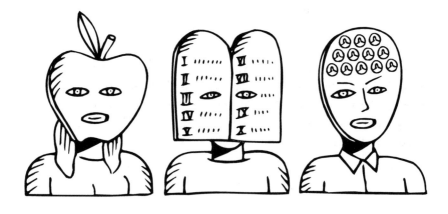

could include the scales of justice; a Samson mask could include long hair; an Esther mask could include a crown and jewels; a Jesus mask could include a crown of thorns and a tear; and a Judas mask could include thirty silver coins.

Encourage kids to be creative. When kids have made their masks, have them wear them for the rest of the meeting or party. Encourage kids to stay in "character" as much as possible.

PARADE OF GHOSTS

Overview: Kids will attempt to identify various characters from history by one object that makes them famous.

Game Type: Quiet, suitable for disabled

Group Size: 10 to 20

Time Involved: 10 to 20 minutes

Supplies: A sheet and the following items for the "ghost" to display (or items that better fit your group):
- Joseph's multicolored coat
- David's slingshot
- Abraham Lincoln's tall black hat
- Benjamin Franklin's kite and key
- Alexander Graham Bell's old telephone
- Thomas Edison's light bulb
- Santa Claus' red and white Christmas hat

Preparation: Recruit a volunteer to wear a sheet and be the "ghost." Have the ghost set up all the items outside the meeting area so kids won't see the items ahead of time.

Have kids form two teams.

Say: **In just a minute, a ghost will appear holding an object that made him or her famous. Talk with your team members. As soon as you think you know who the ghost is, yell out the answer. If you're right, you win the object the ghost is holding. The team with the most ghostly objects at the end of the game wins.**

Have the ghost bring out one item at a time. After the ghost has displayed all the items, declare the team with the most items the most ghoulish.

PUMPKIN HUNT

Overview: Kids will follow a path of small pumpkins.

Game Type: Food, night, outside, suitable for disabled

Group Size: Any

Time Involved: 30 to 45 minutes

Supplies: Small pumpkins, a marker, candy, and flashlights

Preparation: Place several bags of candy outside in a hidden location, such as behind a tree. Then write easy clues on the bottom of each small pumpkin that will guide the group from the meeting area to the candy. Place the pumpkins in their locations.

Inside the meeting area, give kids the first pumpkin and several flashlights. Have kids figure out the clue and then find the second pumpkin, then the third, and so on, until they find the candy.

VARIATION

As a lower-cost alternative, write the clues on construction paper cut into pumpkin shapes.

As an exciting alternative, have an outside party set up at the final destination, complete with lanterns, pumpkin carving, snacks, punch, and even a piñata for kids to break open.

SCREAM

Overview: Kids will try to scare each other into screaming.

Game Type: Night

Group Size: Any

Time Involved: 10 to 20 minutes

Supplies: A whistle

Preparation: Decide which rooms kids will be able to use. Clear away obstacles from those rooms that could hurt the kids or that kids could break.

Have kids play this game in the dark. Turn off all the lights, and keep everything dark. Have kids form two teams: the screamers and the hiders. Explain that the hiders will hide and then try to make the screamers scream. Be sure kids understand that they may not touch anyone else in any way.

Each hider should hide all alone in a room, either behind a door or under a table. Then the screamers should fan out around the building. Their goal is to find the hiders without screaming. If a screamer screams, he or she has to become a hider and try to scare screamers. If screamers don't scream when they find a hider, the hider has to become a screamer and search for hiders.

Have kids play for a certain amount of time. After time is up, see how many kids are on both teams. The team with more players wins. Afterward, have teams switch roles.

Here are some suggestions to keep the game fun and safe.

- Station adults around the playing area to make sure no couples head off together.
- Establish a no-running rule. If someone is caught running, he or she must stand with an adult during that round.
- Have kids play each round for five minutes. When time is up, blow a whistle so everyone will gather back at the starting place.

VARIATION

Have kids play this game in a wooded area with a lot of trees or bushes. Before the game, clear away dangerous obstacles, such as broken glass. Play with the same rules.

SPOOK TAG

Overview: Kids will try to avoid the "great spook."

Game Type: Funny, no supplies and no preparation

Group Size: Any

Time Involved: 2 to 10 minutes

Supplies: None

Preparation: None

Explain to the kids that you will select one person to be the "great spook." Kids, including the great spook, will walk around with their arms extended "Frankenstein-style" and their eyes closed. As they bump into each other, they say "boo." If they say "boo" and hear no response, they know they've run into the great spook and must now join its unearthly band. The player may open his or her eyes and stand so the great spook's hands are now on his or her shoulders. Those who touch the person at the front of the great spook's unearthly band must join the band. The rest just follow behind. If someone bumps into the unearthly band, the band moans, but the player does not have to join them. Play continues until all players have been absorbed into the great spook's unearthly band.

Veterans Day

Peace—In a Moment

Overview: Kids will have a better understanding of the World War I armistice, that moment when "guns fell silent."

Game Type: Active, discussion-starter, knowledge-builder, messy, suitable for disabled

Group Size: Any

Time Involved: 10 to 20 minutes

Supplies: Scrap paper, perhaps paper from the church's recycle bin

Preparation: This game would be most powerful for your group if you can arrange to play it 10:45 a.m. and call for armistice exactly at 11 a.m.

Gather kids together and ask:

● **Does anyone know the history of Veterans Day?**

Say: **We are going to re-enact what happened on the day we now celebrate as Veterans Day.**

Have kids form two teams. Give each team equal amounts of paper to wad up as ammunition.

Say: **We're going to have our own little war. Your job is to hit as many enemy soldiers with paper wads as possible without getting hit yourself. If you get hit, you must sit down because you're dead. We'll continue until I yell the word "armistice," which will occur exactly at 11 a.m. At that point, every one must drop their paper wads and stand perfectly silent and still. Those who fail to do so will lose the war for their team. On your mark, get set, go!**

At exactly 11 a.m., call out: **Armistice!** Then gather your kids together, and read aloud the following quote:

"**We have only movies and books to tell us of the horror of trench warfare in World War I. Grit, slime, unburied corpses in the barb wire,** lice, filth, rats and suicidal forays mixed with the stink and the gut-wrenching fear that is all war— it all ended at an agreed moment, the moment of the Armistice in 1918.

"At 11 a.m. on the 11th day of the 11th month, the guns fell silent" (Gene Marine, "Another American holiday with forgotten origins," San Francisco Examiner, Nov. 10, 1997).

Lead your kids into a discussion about the importance of remembering the origins of holidays and celebrating moments such as armistice.

VARIATION

Ask an older member of your congregation or community—one who actually remembers the first Armistice Day—to visit your group and share what it felt like to be alive an hour after the fighting had ceased.

THANKSGIVING

BOWLING FOR TURKEYS

Overview: Kids will use frozen turkeys to bowl down water-filled two-liter bottles.

Game Type: Funny, suitable for disabled

Group Size: 10 to 20

Time Involved: 45 to 60 minutes

Supplies: A wrapped frozen turkey, ten two-liter bottles, water, masking tape, paper, and pens

Preparation: Fill the bottles with water and close them again. In a room without carpeting, line up the two-liter bottles like a set of ten bowling pins. Use masking tape to create a bowling lane.

LEADER TIP

You may want to have someone stay down at the end of the lane to bring the turkey back to the bowlers.

You may also want to give some silly "turkey" award to the winning team. Have fun, and make the prize as silly as you can.

Have kids form bowling teams of five, and give each team paper and a pen. Have teams set up their score cards with one frame per person.

Kids should hold the frozen turkey by the handle on the wrapping and roll the turkeys down the lanes, attempting to knock down the "pins." Have kids take turns and keep score to see which teams win the "best turkey-bowler" award.

Be sure to either donate the turkey to the church or use it yourself. A frozen turkey can withstand the bumps from a few trips down the "bowling lane."

CORNSTALKS

Overview: Kids will form giant cornstalks by tossing popcorn onto long strips of wide masking tape.

Game Type: Active, funny, messy, suitable for disabled

Group Size: Any

Time Involved: 2 to 10 minutes

Supplies: Wide masking tape, popped popcorn, and small cups or bowls

Preparation: Tear tape into strips one to two feet in length. Place an equal amount of popcorn in the cups.

Have kids form teams of four to six. Select one person from each team to serve as a "cornstalk." Hand each cornstalk several pieces of tape, and ask cornstalks to attach tape strips to their bodies sticky-side out. This can be done easily by turning under the ends about two inches and sticking the tape to the shirt or pants. Ask team members to help the cornstalks so that tape is both in front and back. Suggest that kids avoid sticking tape directly to skin.

Have the cornstalks stand side by side in a single-file line in the center of the room. Then have each team form two groups, with one group at opposite ends of the room.

Hand a popcorn-filled cup to one of each team's players at one end of the room. Explain that each player is to run quickly to other side, tossing a piece of popcorn onto the "cornstalk" along the way.

Point out that players may toss only one piece of popcorn per trip. If it sticks to the tape, the team scores one point. If it falls to the floor, it doesn't count. Once a piece of popcorn has been tossed, no player can touch it.

When the first players reach the opposite side of the room, they should give the cup to a teammate, who continues the relay by running back across the room and tossing a piece of popcorn.

Start the game, and continue until the cups are empty. The team whose cornstalk is wearing the most popcorn is the winner.

Repeat game by gathering the fallen popcorn and having players switch roles. To be fair, make sure teams have the same amount of popcorn before each round.

GOBBLERS!

Overview: Kids will work in teams to form "human turkeys."

Game Type: Active, funny, no supplies and no preparation

Group Size: 30 to 50

Time Involved: 2 to 10 minutes

Supplies: None

Preparation: None

Have kids form teams of six. Explain that each team's members will create a "human turkey" by each acting as a different turkey part. Have team members choose from the following turkey parts:

- The "body" stands in the middle of the group and yells, "Gobble! Gobble!"
- The "left wing" stands to the left of the body and flaps his or her left arm like a chicken.
- The "right wing" stands to the right of the body and flaps his or her right arm like a chicken.
- The "left foot" sits cross-legged to the left of the body.
- The "right foot" sits cross-legged to the right of the body.
- The "tail" stands with his or her back to the body and leans forward at the waist.

When all team members have selected body parts, ask everyone to sit. Explain that on the signal, teams are to see which can be first in forming their "human turkey." Add that as soon as the "turkey" is formed, the whole team should start yelling, "Gobble! Gobble!" as loudly as possible. Since teams will be working pretty fast, this will help determine the winner.

Play a few rounds until group members have gotten the hang of the game. Then have team members switch turkey parts and play again.

MONTHS OF THANKS

Overview: Kids will think of things to be thankful for each month of the year.

Game Type: Icebreaker, quiet, suitable for disabled

Group Size: 20 to 30

Time Involved: 10 to 20 minutes

Supplies: Paper, pencils, and a watch

Preparation: None

Ask students to form teams of four to six, and distribute several sheets of paper and a pencil to each team. Tell kids to choose one team member to write, and explain that they'll have thirty seconds to write down things to be thankful for that happened in the month of January. Then they'll have ten seconds to choose the most original thing on their list. Points will be awarded for each item on their list, with an additional fifty points if their original item is different from other teams' original items. Allow teams to keep track of their own score.

Continue until teams have worked their way through the year.

Musical Thanksgiving

Overview: Kids will answer questions about the first Thanksgiving with musical responses.

Game Type: Funny, musical, suitable for disabled

Group Size: Any

Time Involved: 10 to 20 minutes

Supplies: Paper and a pen

Preparation: Prepare a list of questions about the first Thanksgiving. (See the following examples.)

Have kids form two teams, and explain that you're going to read a Thanksgiving question. Each team must huddle together and think of a song that will work as an answer to the question. Tell kids that answers don't have to be strictly accurate, but they must logically answer the question and be a real line from a real song. For example, if you ask, "Where was the first Thanksgiving dinner eaten?" a team could sing, "Over the river and through the wood." Make sure kids know that their answers must be "rated G." The first team to stand together and sing a response will earn ten points. The team with the highest number of points after ten questions wins.

Following is a list of potential questions:

- Where was the first Thanksgiving dinner eaten?
- How did the guests arrive?
- What were they wearing?
- When did they eat?
- What was the main dish?
- What kind of drinks did they have?
- What did they have for dessert?
- What happened after the meal?
- How did they say goodbye?
- How did they feel about the meal?

PIG OUT!

Overview: Kids will feed each other in an unusual way.

Game Type: Food, funny, messy, suitable for disabled

Group Size: Any

Time Involved: 2 to 10 minutes

Supplies: Napkins and M&M's, popcorn, peanuts, and fish-shaped crackers

Preparation: None

Have kids form pairs and choose who will be the "pig" and who will be the "chef." Give each pig a napkin to tuck under his or her chin. Then have each chef load his or her napkin with M&Ms, popcorn, peanuts, and fish-shaped crackers.

Have the partners line up, facing each other and about five feet apart from each other.

Say: **On my signal the chef will throw the pig one piece of food. If the pig catches the food in the mouth, the pair is still in the game. If the pig doesn't catch the food in the mouth, the pair is out. Each time the pig catches a piece of food, each partner should take one step back on my signal.** We'll see who the "master chef" and "piggiest pigs" are!

> **VARIATION**
>
> For a really messy, hilarious Thanksgiving game, have kids toss mashed potatoes, Jell-O, and canned cranberry salad.

Start the game, and give signals for the pairs to step back and to throw until only one pair remains.

ROUND OF THANKS

Overview: Kids will say what they're thankful for and try to remember what others are thankful for.

Game Type: Affirmation, icebreaker, no supplies and no preparation, quiet, suitable for disabled

Group Size: 20 to 30

Time Involved: 10 to 20 minutes

Supplies: None

Preparation: None

Have kids sit in a circle. Explain that group members are each to share one thing they're thankful for. Add that kids can't repeat what anyone else has said. Encourage players to listen well and remember what everyone says.

When everyone has shared, ask the group to shift one spot to the right. Players must now state what the person who *was* sitting in that spot was thankful for.

Say: **If you can't remember, you must approach that person and tell him or her one thing you like about that person—"You remind me to do my best," for example.**

For the next round, ask kids to shift four seats to the left and play again. Then ask everyone to change seats with someone across the circle. In the new seating order, see if players can remember what the original occupants of the seats were thankful for. Finally, see who can name what each group member is thankful for. Again, if someone can't remember, he or she must make an affirming remark to the person.

SOCK-O-PLENTY

Overview: Kids will try to stuff items into a tube sock.

Game Type: Active, discussion-starter, suitable for disabled

Group Size: Any

Time Involved: 2 to 10 minutes

Supplies: Clean tube socks and a watch

Preparation: None

Have kids form teams of four to six. Give each team one tube sock. Explain that teams will have twenty seconds to stuff as many personal items as possible into their tube socks. Items might include a watch, comb, wallet, bracelet, or lipstick. Add that the goal is to get as many items as possible into the sock; it doesn't matter if the items are the same.

Start the game, and call time after twenty seconds. See which team stuffed the most items, and declare it a winner for that round.

Play another round in which teams have thirty seconds to collect the most *different* personal items into their socks. Emphasize the fact that two items may not be alike. Call time after thirty seconds, and declare a winner.

The final round calls for teams to see how many different *room* items they can stuff into their socks. Emphasize that no one may use personal items during this round, but anything in the room is fair game. Allow two minutes for this round. Then call time and declare a winner.

After playing three rounds, lead a discussion on giving thanks by asking:

- **Was there anything frustrating about this activity? Explain.**
- **Which was easier: collecting personal items or finding things from around the room?**
- **Is it easier or more difficult to give thanks for things we can easily see rather than for things that take time to locate? Explain.**

STUFF THE TURKEY

Overview: Kids will use inflated balloons to fill trash bags worn by team members.

Game Type: Active, funny, suitable for disabled

Group Size: Any

Time Involved: 10 to 20 minutes

Supplies: Large plastic trash bags, scissors, balloons, and a watch

Preparation: Cut two leg holes in the bottom of each trash bag. You'll need one trash bag for each team of four to six.

Have kids form teams of four to six. Ask one person from each team to serve as the "turkey" and one to serve as the "farmer." Hand each turkey a prepared plastic trash bag. Ask that turkeys wear the bags as shorts, with legs placed through the holes. Give each farmer several balloons. Hand all the other players one balloon each. Position teams across the room, mixing players from different teams. Once positioned, tell players with balloons that they may not move during play.

Explain that players are to inflate and tie off balloons while turkeys run around and try to "feed." To feed, turkeys must run around so teammates can drop balloons into the trash bags they're wearing. To keep the balloon players supplied, farmers run around and distribute new balloons—but farmers can't feed the turkeys.

Start the game, and call time after three minutes. Declare the team whose turkey has the most balloons the winner.

Play the game several times so other players can serve as turkeys.

Talk Like a Turkey

Overview: Kids will gobble their way through compliments.

Game Type: Affirmation, funny, mixer, suitable for disabled

Group Size: Any

Time Involved: 2 to 10 minutes

Supplies: Craft feathers (from craft stores) or paper feathers and a watch

Preparation: None

Give each group member five feathers. Explain to kids that their goal is to give those five feathers away. To do this, kids must gobble "thank-liments" to each other. A thank-liment can be a reason they're glad to see that person or a reason they're thankful for that person. Add that to gobble a thank-liment, kids must gobble before and after the sentence, but not during the sentence; receivers must understand what is being said. Encourage kids to be specific.

After kids deliver each thank-liment, they must give one feather to that person. Urge students not to avoid compliments, but to out-compliment each other.

Start the game, and give kids about five minutes to race to give away their feathers. Then call time. The kids with the fewest feathers win.

Three-Piece Turkey

Overview: Kids will try to pin turkey parts together while blindfolded.

Game Type: Suitable for disabled

Group Size: Any

Time Involved: 10 to 20 minutes

Supplies: Tape, blindfolds, scissors, and the "Turkey Parts" handout (p. 274)

Preparation: Make photocopies of the "Turkey Parts" handout (p. 274), one copy for each group of three. From each handout, cut out the three turkey parts.

Have kids form teams of three, and give each team a set of turkey parts, tape, and a blindfold. Have kids line up at one end of the room. Explain that the first member of the team will put on the blindfold, carry one turkey part to the opposite end of the room, tape the turkey part to the wall, and then return to the team. Then the next teammate will put on the blindfold and tape the next turkey part to the wall, and then the last teammate will repeat the process. When all three team members have returned, the team should sit down and wait for others to finish.

Start the race. When everyone has finished, award ten points to the team that finished first and twenty points to the team with the best turkey. Then have teams play again. The first team to reach fifty points wins.

TURKEY PARTS

TURKEY IN THE STRAW

Overview: Kids will find "turkey beaks" hidden in a pile of straw.

Game Type: Active, funny, messy, outside, suitable for disabled

Group Size: Any

Time Involved: 10 to 20 minutes

Supplies: Hay (from a feed store) or a lot of shredded paper, a package of candy corn, a cassette player with batteries, and a recording of the song "Turkey in the Straw"

Preparation: Put the hay outside in a large pile, and then sprinkle in the package of candy corn.

> **LEADER TIP**
>
> If you'd rather have kids play this game inside, you can place trash bags or newspaper on the floor for easy cleanup, or you can have your kids clean up by making it part of the game.

Have kids form a large circle around the hay. Have them pay close attention to who is standing on either side of them.

Say: **This game is a combination of the old song "Turkey in the Straw" and the maxim "You can't find a needle in a haystack." You don't have to find a needle, but you do have to find a turkey beak (candy corn), hold it up to your nose, and return to your exact place in the circle. We're successful when everyone is back in place.**

Play the music to start the game. Every once in a while, stop the music; then have kids freeze where they are and gobble. They may begin searching again when the music starts again.

> **LEADER TIP**
>
> If you don't have a recording of "Turkey in the Straw," have kids play the game without stopping to gobble.

If you have a small group, you may want to have players find more than one piece of candy corn each round.

TURKEY TROT

Overview: Kids will try to blow feathers across a finish line.

Game Type: Active

Group Size: Any

Time Involved: 2 to 10 minutes

Supplies: Craft feathers (from craft stores) or paper feathers

Preparation: None

Have kids form two teams, and have teams line up behind a starting line. Designate a finish line at the other end of the playing area.

At your starting signal, players will throw their feathers into the air and try to blow them across the finish line. If a feather drops to the floor, the player should pick it up, take three giant steps backward, and then continue toward the finish line.

Depending on your group size, you can score the game in several ways. If your group is small, have all players blow their feathers at once. As players cross the finish line, have them quickly sit down together. The first team with all players seated wins. If your group is large, have team members blow their feathers in relay fashion. The first team with all players across the finish line wins.

WEAR THE WATTLE

Overview: Kids will try to attach a "wattle" to a "turkey" while blindfolded.

Game Type: Funny, suitable for disabled

Group Size: 10 to 20

Time Involved: 10 to 20 minutes

Supplies: Three knee-high nylon stockings, masking tape, and blindfolds

Preparation: Attach a three-inch piece of masking tape to each knee-high stocking.

First explain to the kids that the red piece of skin that hangs from a turkey's throat is called a wattle. Choose three kids to be "turkeys" and three to be "wattlers." Have the turkeys stand about five feet apart from each other. Then have each wattler stand about ten feet away from a turkey, and hand each wattler a knee-high stocking "wattle." Ask the rest of the kids to form three groups, each group sitting on the floor to the side of a turkey. Blindfold the wattlers. Explain that the wattlers will each need to tape a wattle as close to a turkey's throat as possible.

Say: **The turkeys must remain silent, and the wattlers can't use their hands to feel where the wattle should go; the rest of you will help your wattler. If your wattler is getting closer to the right spot, you should say, "Gobble, gobble." But if your wattler getting further away, you should shout, "Turk! Turk! Turk!"**

Remind the wattlers to approach the turkeys gently and without sudden movements. Spin the wattlers a few time to confuse them, and then begin the game. After each wattler has taped a wattle on a turkey, have wattlers remove their blindfolds to compare results. Then continue playing, giving other kids chances to be the turkeys and wattlers.

CHRISTMAS

ALL WRAPPED UP

Overview: Kids will work together to demonstrate their creative wrapping abilities.

Game Type: Funny, suitable for disabled

Group Size: Any

Time Involved: 10 to 20 minutes

Supplies: Several rolls of wrapping paper, bows, tape, ribbon, scissors

Preparation: None

Have kids form teams of four, and then have them choose one team member to be the "gift."

Say: **I want to see how creative the rest of you can be at wrapping your gifts. You'll have ten minutes to create the most creative, funny, or ugly package for the rest of the group to enjoy.**

Start the game, and then call time after ten minutes. Have the groups vote on the best award for each team.

BOOTY TOSS

Overview: Kids will take aim with candy in order to win it all.

Game Type: Food, suitable for disabled

Group Size: 10 to 20

Time Involved: 2 to 10 minutes

Supplies: A ladder; a boot; a watch; and bags of several different kinds of individually wrapped candies, such as cinnamon disks, small candy canes, chocolate kisses, and caramels

Preparation: Place the ladder in the middle of the room, and put the boot on top of the ladder.

Have kids form teams of four. Every team should have the same number of players, so you may need to play, too. Have teams gather around the ladder. Give each team a different type of candy to distribute among the team members. For example, one team will receive only cinnamon disks, and another team will receive only caramels.

Explain that when you say "go," kids will have thirty seconds to toss as much candy as possible into the boot without touching the ladder.

Say: **Although everyone will be tossing candy at the same time, each person may toss one piece of candy at a time.**

Explain that the team that gets the most candy into the boot will get to keep all the candy from the boot.

When everyone understands how to play, say: **Go!** Give kids thirty seconds to throw the candy, and then call time. Retrieve the boot, and count how many pieces of each type of candy are in the boot. Give the team with the most pieces of candy all the candy from the boot.

Have teams collect their pieces of candy from the floor, and play again until all the candy has been won.

CANDY CANE HORSESHOES

Overview: Kids will play a simple Christmas version of horseshoes.

Game Type: Suitable for disabled

Group Size: 2 to 10

Time Involved: 2 to 10 minutes

Supplies: A Christmas tree and candy canes

Preparation: None

Have kids circle around the Christmas tree and then stand about ten feet away from it. Give each person ten candy canes, and tell kids they get one point for every candy cane they manage to hook onto the tree. However, the only way they can hook a candy cane on the tree is to toss it underhand.

Start the game. When everyone has thrown their candy canes, declare the person who hooked the most canes the winner. Let kids play several times.

CAROL STAGERS

Overview: Kids will act out Christmas songs sung by group members.

Game Type: Active, funny, musical, no supplies and no preparation, suitable for disabled

Group Size: 30 to 50

Time Involved: 10 to 20 minutes

Supplies: None

Preparation: None

Have kids form teams of four to six, and have teams spread across the floor. Ask everyone to sit. Explain that a volunteer is going to sing a favorite Christmas song. While singing, he or she will stop occasionally and point to any team. Then that team must act out the word or phrase the singer just sang until the singer chooses to continue—which could be some time!

Encourage singers to keep players on their toes by pointing to teams as fast and as often as possible. Use as many volunteer singers as possible.

VARIATION

As a twist, have singers close their eyes and turn clockwise while singing. When the singer stops turning and points, the team he or she is pointing to gets to perform.

A CHRISTMAS GIFT

Overview: Kids will experience the joy of giving while they listen to the Christmas story.

Game Type: Bible, discussion-starter, quiet, suitable for disabled

Group Size: Any

Time Involved: 10 to 20 minutes

Supplies: Bibles, one small gift for each group member, wrapping paper, tape, boxes, and scissors. Gifts should be very inexpensive and very similar to each other.

Preparation: Wrap each gift. If possible, wrap the gifts in identical boxes.

Have kids sit in a circle. Distribute the gifts you purchased and wrapped, but instruct kids not to open their presents. Explain that you're going to read aloud the Christmas story. Say: As I read, pass your gift to the person on your right every time I read the words "God," "Lord," and "Jesus."

Read aloud Luke 1:26-38; 2:1-20; and Matthew 2:1-12. Afterward, ask:

- **What did you have to do to receive the gift that was passed to you?**
- **Did anyone not want a gift?**
- **How does it make you feel to know that Christ's gift to *you* is everlasting life?**

Tell the kids that they can now open and enjoy their gifts!

CHRISTMAS HOCKEY

Overview: Kids will play hockey with candy canes and chocolate kisses.

Game Type: Suitable for disabled

Group Size: Any

Time Involved: 2 to 10 minutes

Supplies: Chocolate kisses and candy canes

Preparation: None

Have kids form pairs, and have each pair find a table or a three-foot area of the floor on which to play the game. Give each pair two candy canes and five chocolate kisses.

Say: **Each person will need to mark off a goal area with two chocolate kisses. If your opponent is able to hit the chocolate kiss "puck" through your chocolate kisses, he or she scores one point.**

To begin the game, put the puck in the middle of your playing area. You may use only your candy canes as hockey sticks. If you touch the puck with anything but the candy cane, your opponent gets a point. Whoever reaches ten points first wins.

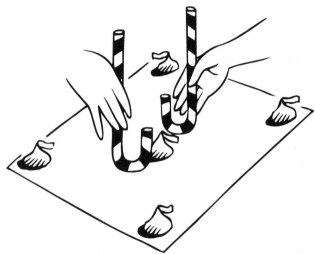

When everyone understands the rules, begin the game. Have the kids play several rounds, or have the winners play each other until you have a Christmas hockey champion.

CHRISTMAS SNOW RACE

Overview: Kids will find out how snow affects their Three-Legged Race.

Game Type: Active, outside, winter

Group Size: Any

Time Involved: 2 to 10 minutes

Supplies: Christmas stockings or ribbon

Preparation: None

Have kids form pairs, and hand each pair a Christmas stocking or ribbon. Then have kids line up outside in the snow, and indicate a starting line and a finish line. Have each pair tie two of their legs together just below the knee.

Say: **Ready? Go!**

Declare the first pair to finish the winners. Let kids play several times until they get used to running a Three-Legged Race in the snow.

GIFT-EXCHANGE GAME

Overview: Kids will play a game to exchange Christmas gifts.

Game Type: Discussion-starter, quiet, suitable for disabled

Group Size: Any

Time Involved: 10 to 20 minutes

Supplies: A watch and a couple of inexpensive, wrapped gifts in case a student forgets to bring one or in case you have visitors

Preparation: Have kids each wrap an inexpensive gag gift— something they have at home or something they purchase for less than two dollars—that will be suitable for either a guy or a girl. Explain that they should wrap the gift in such a way that no one will have any idea what's inside.

Have kids sit in a circle together, and pile all the gifts in the center of the room. Tell kids that they'll get to choose a gift in order from the oldest group member to the youngest group member.

One person at a time may choose a gift from the pile. That person, however, can't pick up a gift or shake it before making choice. If a person touches a gift, that's the gift he or she has to take. Let each person take a turn choosing a gift. However, emphasize that kids can't open their gifts yet. They simply must set their gifts down in from of them.

After everyone has chosen a gift, explain that kids have two minutes to try to trade their gifts with others. Call time after the two minutes, and have everyone sit in the circle again with the gift in front of him or her.

One at a time, beginning with the oldest person and moving to the youngest person, have kids open their gifts. Afterward, ask:

- Why did you choose the gift from the pile that you did?
- In what ways were you surprised or fooled by your gift when you opened it?
- What's fun about giving and receiving gifts?
- When God gave us the gift of Jesus, why do you think people were excited?

O Christmas Tree

Overview: Kids will decorate human "Christmas trees."

Game Type: Active, funny, suitable for disabled

Group Size: Any

Time Involved: 2 to 10 minutes

Supplies: Red and green crepe paper and tape

Preparation: None

Have kids form two teams, and have each team choose someone to be the team's human "Christmas tree." Have teams line up on one side of the room, and have the trees stand at the other side of the room and face the teams.

Give the first player of one team a roll of red crepe paper and some tape, and give the first player of the other team a roll of green crepe paper and some tape.

At your signal, the first player from each team should run to the tree, attach a length of crepe paper to the tree's neck or shoulder, and then stretch the crepe paper at an angle down to the floor and securely tape it. Then the player should run back to the team, hand the roll of crepe paper and tape to the next player, and sit down.

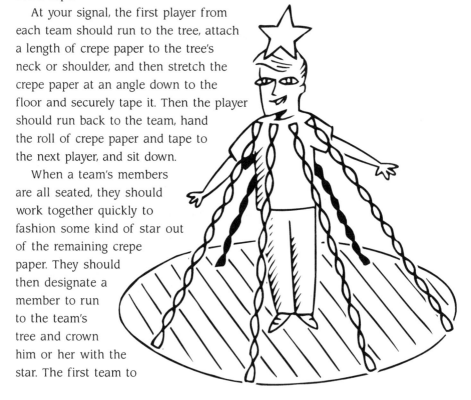

When a team's members are all seated, they should work together quickly to fashion some kind of star out of the remaining crepe paper. They should then designate a member to run to the team's tree and crown him or her with the star. The first team to place a star on its tree wins.

Caution kids not to harm the tree's clothing with the tape. Crepe paper can be tied loosely around the neck or arms if tape poses a problem.

O TANNENBOOM

Overview: Kids will systematically destroy a used Christmas tree.

Game Type: Active, funny, outside, senior high, suitable for disabled

Group Size: 2 to 10

Time Involved: 30 to 45 minutes

Supplies: Masking tape or yellow string, disposable ornaments, a used Christmas tree from a dumpster or curb, and whatever you intend to shoot at the tree. (See below.) Tin cans work well as ornaments, as do disposable aluminum pans and anything else that will make a sound.

Preparation: Set up and decorate the Christmas tree.

Christmas is past and, other than credit card bills, what's left? Tons of used Christmas trees, *that's* what! Put one to good use with a rousing game of O Tannenboom!

Have kids stand at least thirty feet away from the Christmas tree and shoot at it with one of the following items:

- **Nerf "blasters"**—Foam products make shooting at the tree safe anywhere.
- **Snowballs or other balls**—This version gets kids outside, and they may decide to "accidentally" aim the snowballs at something other than the tree.
- **Rolls of toilet paper**—This version allows kids to create a neat visual effect—toilet paper streamers floating in the air.

Create a firing line with tape on the floor, or use a piece of yellow string if you're outside. Observe all appropriate safety rules. Give kids turns calling their shots and firing at the tree. If so inclined, assign point values to specific ornaments—"100 points for knocking the Barbie doll off the top of the tree," for example.

Remember to say, "Don't try this at home, kids."

OUTSMART THE CRUSHERS

Overview: Kids will sculpt Christmas "crushers" and name ways to bolster Christmas cheer.

Game Type: Affirmation, discussion-starter, quiet, suitable for disabled

Group Size: 2 to 10

Time Involved: 10 to 20 minutes

Supplies: Modeling dough

Preparation: None

Give each group member a lump of modeling dough, and direct kids to shape it into a Christmas "crusher"—something that gets in the way of their Christmas happiness—for example, a relationship, an attitude, a circumstance, commercialization, or a time pressure. Your students may look at you blankly, but assure them that you want to hear what they have to say.

After a few minutes, ask each group member to display and explain his or her crusher. Be sure to compliment each person for his or her wisdom. Lead the kids into a discussion about the struggles they face in honoring Jesus during Christmas.

After a bit of discussion, ask kids to reshape their dough crusher into an action or attitude with which they can restore Christmas joy to themselves and others. Again, give kids a few minutes to work, and then ask them to display and explain their sculptures. As they share, ask:

- **How does your action or attitude honor Jesus?**
- **What tip would you offer to help others find joy at Christmastime?**

POP A CHARADE

Overview: Kids will form shapes of Christmas items as a group.

Game Type: Active, funny, suitable for disabled

Group Size: 10 to 20

Time Involved: 20 to 30 minutes

Supplies: Red and green balloons, a pen, and slips of paper

Preparation: On the slips of paper, write the names of Christmas-related objects that groups of kids could form in a game of Charades—candy cane, nativity scene, Christmas tree, and snowman, for example. Then insert the slips of paper into the balloons, and inflate and tie off the balloons.

Have kids form two teams: the red team and the green team. Explain that teams will take turns popping balloons and finding slips of paper inside. When a team finds the slip of paper, team members must work together to act out or form the item named on the slip of paper. Then the other team has to guess what's being formed. For example, if the red team pops a balloon and finds the slip of paper with the words "candy cane" written on it, team members must link together and form a candy cane shape. Then the other team has to guess what's being formed.

Have teams take turns until they've used all the clues.

Rapid Wrap

Overview: Kids will wrap a box as many times as possible in two minutes.

Game Type: Suitable for disabled

Group Size: 10 to 20

Time Involved: 2 to 10 minutes

Supplies: Boxes of similar size, wrapping paper or newspaper, tape, scissors, ribbon, and a watch

Preparation: None

Have kids form teams of four. Give each team a box, wrapping paper, tape, scissors, and ribbon. Explain that teams will have two minutes to wrap their box as many times as possible using the provided materials. Add that each layer must include paper, tape, and ribbon.

Start the game. Call time after two minutes, and have teams take turns unwrapping their boxes. Declare the team with the most layers the winner.

Repeat the game, but challenge kids to neatly wrap their boxes without tape.

Rudolph Relay

Overview: Kids will race carrying maraschino cherries between their lips and noses.

Game Type: Active, funny, suitable for disabled

Group Size: Any

Time Involved: 2 to 10 minutes

Supplies: Paper plates and maraschino cherries

Preparation: Place six cherries on each plate. You'll need one plate for every team of six.

Have kids form teams of six. Designate a starting line and a finish line, and have teams line up in single file at the starting line. Place a plate of cherries on the floor in front of each team. Explain that players each must hold a cherry under their noses with only their upper lips. They may not use their hands at any time during the relay.

On "go," the first player in each team must load his or her cherry and proceed to the goal line and back, then eat the cherry. The second player may not begin until the first player has swallowed the cherry. The first team to finish wins.

Santa and the Elves

Overview: Kids will offer each other verbal gifts.

Game Type: Affirmation, mixer, quiet, suitable for disabled

Group Size: Any

Time Involved: 2 to 10 minutes

Supplies: Slips of paper, a pen, and a hat or bag

Preparation: Fold enough small slips of paper for each person to have one; mark one with an X.

Allow everyone to draw a slip of paper out of the hat, instructing them not to share with anyone what's on their paper. Tell kids that the person who received an X is Santa and everyone else is an elf.

Say: **When I say "go," everyone should mingle and whisper Christmas greetings. The elves will whisper, "Merry Christmas," but Santa will offer personal verbal gifts, such as "Susan, I'm so glad you're here tonight" or "Joe, you're a great friend." Once Santa gives you a verbal gift, you also become Santa and begin giving verbal gifts to others. We'll continue until everyone has become a Santa.**

SANTA'S WHISKERS

Overview: Teams will create the longest beard possible out of shaving cream.

Game Type: Funny, messy, suitable for disabled

Group Size: Any

Time Involved: 2 to 10 minutes

Supplies: Cans of shaving cream and plastic garbage bags

Preparation: None

Have kids form groups of four to six, and give each team a can of shaving cream and two trash bags. Select one to three players in each group to be the "singers," one to be the "elf barber," one to be "Santa," and one to be "Santa's wife." Have the elf barbers take the cans of shaving cream and the singers take the plastic bags and stand at one end of the room; have all the Santas and their wives stand at the other end of the room.

On your cue, the singers must sing out "Here Comes Santa Claus," and the Santas must run to stand on one of the plastic bags. Then the elf barbers must cover their Santas' chests with the second plastic bags and use the shaving cream to create the longest beards they can for their Santas.

The Santas' wives must continue to stand at the start lines and shout, "Say it, dear! Say it!" When an elf barber has finished the beard, the Santa must turn to face Santa's wife, stand up straight and tall, and say, "Ho! Ho! Ho!" The beard must stay intact during the belly laugh. If a beard falls off, the elf barber must recreate it, and Santa's wife must repeat her line again. The team whose Santa can say "Ho! Ho! Ho!" with the longest beard remaining intact is the winner.

SERVICE SNACKS

Overview: Kids will prepare and deliver Christmas treats.

Game Type: Food, service, suitable for disabled

Group Size: 10 to 20

Time Involved: More than 1 hour

Supplies: Bibles, paper, wrapping paper, tape, scissors, markers, and supplies and facilities to cook an easy item such as slice-and-bake cookies

Preparation: Plan to have the group gather in the church kitchen or at a home to cook a snack. Also recruit a couple of volunteers to drive kids to deliver the snacks.

Ask group members to name adults and children who make church wonderful for them. For example, perhaps an adult always smiles when they walk into worship, or a child works hard in Sunday school. Also ask kids to think of people in the church who could use some cheering up.

Then ask the kids to help prepare a Christmas treat to deliver to these families. Assign some kids to cook, some to wrap the treats, and some to make cards for everyone in the group to sign. While the treats are baking, have kids look in Bibles and brainstorm for statements to write on the cards—statements that celebrate both that person and Jesus' birth. Here are some possibilities:

- Thanks for being "church" to us.
- When you smile, I see Jesus in you.
- Your humble attitude reminds us not to call attention to ourselves.

Then add a Bible verse such as Colossians 2:5 to each card. Ask:

- **How does preparing treats show someone that you care?**
- **How does putting your appreciation into words show someone that you care?**
- **How can we remember to care for others all year?**

When the treats are ready and wrapped, have kids either drive the treats to the families or deliver them at the next church service.

SNOWBALL ATTACK

Overview: Kids will throw paper "snowballs" at each other.

Game Type: Active, suitable for disabled

Group Size: 30 to 50

Time Involved: 2 to 10 minutes

Supplies: A watch and scrap paper, perhaps paper from the church's recycle bin

Preparation: None

Have kids form two teams, and have teams gather at opposite ends of the room. Declare the middle area of the room "off limits." Then give each team stacks of scrap paper.

Say: **We're going to have an indoor "snowball" fight. Use the paper to make "snowballs," and then throw the snowballs into the other team's territory. You can also deflect incoming snowballs, but only by batting at them with your open hand. Once a snowball lands, you can't touch it. You'll play for three minutes, and then we'll count how many snowballs made it into enemy territory.**

Start the game, and call time after three minutes have passed. Have teams count the snowballs in their territory, and declare the team that success-fully threw the most snowballs the winner.

VARIATION

Of course, kids will love to play this game outside with real snow!

STUFFY SLEIGHS

Overview: Kids will try to throw the most "presents" into "sleighs."

Game Type: Active, suitable for disabled

Group Size: 20 to 30

Time Involved: 2 to 10 minutes

Supplies: Plastic trash bags, a watch, and scrap paper, perhaps paper from the church's recycle bin

Preparation: None

Have kids form teams of three, and give each team a plastic trash bag. One person on each team will be the "sleigh," and this person will hold the trash bag. Have all the sleighs line up at one end of the room, and emphasize that they can't move away from their position during the game. Point out a designated throwing line that's about five feet away from the sleighs. The two people left on each team will be the "elves," and their job will be to fill the sleigh. Have the elves begin at the wall opposite the sleighs. Place scrap paper in the middle of the room.

Explain that an elf must run to the middle of the floor, wad a piece of paper into a ball to create a "gift," and run to the designated throwing line. Without crossing the line, the elf must try to throw the gift into the sleigh and then run back to the other elf, who will repeat the process. Gifts that don't make it into sleighs must stay where they fall, untouched by anyone.

Start the game, and have kids play for three minutes. Then call time, and have sleighs count how many gifts made it into the trash bags. The team with the most number of gifts wins. Have team members switch roles and play again.

End the game by having an all-out "blizzard" in which teams empty their trash bags onto other players. Be sure to have kids clean up the "snow"!

TRIMMERS

Overview: Kids will attempt to decorate a Christmas tree in the dark.

Game Type: Funny, night, suitable for disabled

Group Size: 10 to 20

Time Involved: 10 to 20 minutes

Supplies: A watch; a small artificial Christmas tree or a coat rack; and decorating items, such as tinsel, garland, plastic ornaments, and a tree skirt

Preparation: Set up the Christmas tree in the center of a room. Place tree-trimming decorations on the floor next to the tree.

Gather kids around the tree in the center of the floor, and point out the tree-trimming decorations. Explain that the group will have five minutes to trim the tree as best as possible—with the lights off.

Turn off the lights, and give kids about five minutes to turn the tree into a work of art. After five minutes, call time and turn the lights on. Participants may be surprised at how well they decorated. On the other hand, they may be shocked to find a tree skirt hanging from the tree top.

Give the group thirty seconds to pull everything off the tree. Repeat the game with the girls only. Then repeat with the guys only, and compare the creations.

New Year's Eve

Balloon Bust

Overview: Kids will simulate firecracker pops by popping balloons.

Game Type: Active, funny, night, suitable for disabled

Group Size: Any

Time Involved: 2 to 10 minutes

Supplies: Balloons

Preparation: Inflate the balloons, or have kids help you inflate the balloons just before the game.

Have kids form teams of four. Set the pile of balloons at one end of the room, and have teams line up at the other end.

Say: **Instead of shooting off fireworks to celebrate the new year, we're going to pop balloons.**

Explain that, at midnight, the first person on each team will run to the balloons, sit on a balloon to pop it, pick up the broken balloon, and run back. Then the next person will repeat the process.

Start the game. When the balloons are gone, have teams count their broken balloons. The team with the most broken balloons wins.

Decades Charades

Overview: Kids will act out scenes to represent each decade up to the present.

Game Type: Funny, suitable for disabled

Group Size: 20 to 30

Time Involved: 20 to 30 minutes

Supplies: Slips of paper, a pen, and a hat or bag

Preparation: On the slips of paper, write different decades—
"Fifties," "Sixties," "Seventies," and so on. Based on
how much time you have and your students'
historical knowledge, you can decide how far back
you want to go. The fifties should be an easy
starting place for most teenagers. Fold the slips, and
put them in the hat.

Ask students to form teams of four to six. Choose a team to go first, and
allow the team to select a slip of paper from the basket. Tell team members
that they must act out a scene to represent that decade, and the scene must
involve their whole team. They can talk, sing, use items available in the room,
or do whatever is necessary to help others guess which decade they represent. Since this game is just for fun, there's no reason for others not to guess.

When someone has guessed the team's decade, that team returns their paper to the hat and sits down. Decades may be repeated, but the scene must
be different.

END-OF-YEAR TRIATHLON

Overview: Kids will participate in an Olympic-type event using
ends of household items.

Game Type: Active, suitable for disabled

Group Size: 20 to 30

Time Involved: 30 to 45 minutes

Supplies: Three of each of the following items: empty toilet tissue
rolls, leftover pieces of bar soap, paper cups, trash cans,
towel bars, and toilet-paper-roll holders. You'll also need
one beat-up old towel.

Preparation: Tear the towel into three small pieces.

Explain to the kids that to celebrate the end of the year, they're going to
compete in a triathlon with ends—the end of a roll of toilet paper, the end of
the bar of soap, and the end of the towel.

Have kids form three teams. One player from each team will begin the
event. As soon as a member from one team completes phase one, that person can start phase two, and the second team member can start phase one.

Team members should try to complete each phase quickly and move on to the next. As team members complete phase three, they can sit down and cheer on their teammates. The triathlon is complete when everyone has completed all three phases of the event.

- **Event 1**—For the first phase of the triathlon, you will need empty toilet paper rolls and toilet-paper-roll holders. You'll also need some trash cans as targets.

Teams will compete from various distances to see which team can score the most goals by holding a toilet-paper-roll holder and flinging the empty roll off of it toward the trash can.

Teams can also challenge other teams to a specialty-shot challenge in which they shoot specialty shots—backward over the shoulder, eyes closed, or through the legs, for example.

- **Event 2**—For the second phase of the triathlon, insert the piece of soap in a bathroom cup, and hurl the soap at the goal.
- **Event 3**—For the final phase of the triathlon, use a towel bar to scoop up a piece of towel, hold the bar upright with the towel on top like an Olympic torch, and deposit the bit of towel in the trash can.

The first person to finish all three events earns ten points. The second person earns nine points, and so on. Team members add their individual scores together for the team score, and the team with the highest score wins.

FETTI RESOLUTIONS

Overview: Kids will make confetti from New Year's resolutions.

Game Type: Affirmation, messy, suitable for disabled

Group Size: Any

Time Involved: 2 to 10 minutes

Supplies: Paper, pencils, a watch, and a trash bag or trash can

Preparation: None

Give each person paper and a pencil. Have kids write down three New Year's resolutions as follows: a resolution you *do* intend to keep, a resolution you *do not* intend to keep, and a resolution you made the previous year but *did not keep*.

After about three minutes, call time and allow kids to share what they wrote. See if kids can guess the correct type of resolution after a person shares one.

Ask kids to tear from their paper the one written resolution they intend to keep, fold that piece of paper, and put it in a pocket. Then ask kids to tear the other resolutions into as many pieces as possible.

Then have kids form two lines from one end of the room to the other. Lines should be about five feet apart and should face each other. Explain that each person in the group is going to take part in a special New Year's Eve parade. One at a time, players will walk in between the lines from one side of the room to the other. Along the way, these players will wave and throw kisses while shouting their "intended" resolutions to the rest of the group.

Meanwhile, line players will toss a little "confetti"—their torn resolutions—at the passerby while yelling things like "Hang in there!" "You can do it!" and "I know you can!" Encourage players to add sound effects like whistles and claps. As players move from one end of the room to the other, lines should slide down to make room for players at opposite end.

End the game with a goal to start the year off clean. Have the group resolve to pick up all trash and place it in a trash bag as fast as possible. Make sure kids keep this resolution!

NEW YEAR'S BABY-CHANGING RELAY

Overview: Kids will form a baby-changing station and race to see which team can change the fastest.

Game Type: Active, discussion-starter, funny, messy

Group Size: 10 to 20

Time Involved: 2 to 10 minutes

Supplies: Two adult-size diapers or large cloth dishtowels, two containers of cornstarch or baby powder, and two plastic trash bags

Preparation: At one end of the room, lay out the trash bags. On each trash bag, place a diaper and powder.

<table>
<tr><td>

LEADER TIP

Players must be wearing pants or shorts to participate in this game—no skirts or dresses.

</td><td>

Have kids form two teams. Have the teams line up in single file at the end of the room opposite the supplies.

</td></tr>
</table>

Say: **New Year's is a time to think about making some changes—not necessarily great big changes, but maybe some little baby-sized changes—in what you've been doing. Each of you needs to think of a baby-sized change you need to make during this new year. When it's your turn, run to your team's "changing station," sprinkle some baby powder into the diaper as you shout out your baby-sized change, and put on the diaper. After the diaper is completely on, take it off and leave it there, run back to your team, and tag the next player.**

Select a "change agent" from each team to help the runner at the changing station. The last person on each team will help the change agent perform the task. The team is finished when the change agent returns to the relay line.

When the teams have finished, ask:

- How is this game like or unlike making a real change?
- What is required to change a habit?
- Why do you think there's so much talk about change at New Year's?
- What can you do to help ensure that you really do change the little thing you mentioned during the game?

RESOLUTION READOUT

Overview: Kids will try to guess which resolutions belong to group members.

Game Type: Discussion-starter, quiet, suitable for disabled

Group Size: 2 to 10

Time Involved: 10 to 20 minutes

Supplies: Paper and pencils

Preparation: None

Give one slip of paper and a pencil to each member of your group.

Say: **Please write down one resolution that you'd like to make for New Year's. Then I'll read aloud each resolution, and we'll see if we can guess who it belongs to.**

After the kids have written their resolutions, collect them. Then read each one aloud and ask kids to decide who it belongs to. After they've discussed all the resolutions, ask:

- **What was it like to have the group guess your resolution?**
- **Why are resolutions so hard to keep?**

RESOLVED

Overview: Kids will discover who has the most unique New Year's resolutions.

Game Type: Quiet, suitable for disabled

Group Size: 20 to 30

Time Involved: 20 to 30 minutes

Supplies: Paper and pens

Preparation: None

Have everyone write down three resolutions for the new year. When kids have finished, have them form teams of at least three and compile their resolutions.

Have a team read aloud one resolution. Any other teams that have the same resolution or a very similar resolution should say so, and they all should mark out that resolution. For example, if teams shared the resolutions of "Begin a diet," "Lose weight," or "Eat less junk food," they would all mark out those resolutions. If the other teams don't have that resolution on their lists, the reading team gets to leave the resolution on their list.

Repeat the process until teams have read through all their resolutions. The team with the most resolutions left wins.

TEN YEARS FROM NOW

Overview: Kids will hear possible scenarios of their futures.

Game Type: Funny, quiet, suitable for disabled

Group Size: Any

Time Involved: 2 to 10 minutes

Supplies: Paper and pens

Preparation: None

Have kids sit in a circle. Give each player a sheet of paper and a pen. Tell each person to write his or her own name at the top of the paper and then fold the paper over to cover the name.

Have kids pass the papers to the right. Then have each player write a future date, at least ten years away. Have kids fold and pass the papers again. Repeat the process, having kids write a sentence describing an event, the name of a place, an occupation, the name of a personal possession, a sentence about how a possession was acquired, and a sentence describing the effect the possession has on life.

Depending on the size or creativity of your class, you may want to add categories to keep the game going. Then have kids unfold the papers and each read aloud the story found there.

INDEXES

GAME TYPE

ACTIVE

ICEBREAKER

JUNIOR HIGH

TEAM-BUILDER

10 TO 20 MINUTES